D0847738

This
Book
was placed in the
Church
Library
by

Barbara Bates

you
are
SOMEBODY

you
are
SOMEBODY
ben johnson

FORUM HOUSE/Publishers
Atlanta

1382

contents

The You of the title
is also the I of the author.
Here I share my struggle
to accept and celebrate my own personhood;
at the same time,
I wish to affirm your worth,
and I invite you to begin living
in the confidence that you are
a unique, unrepeatable miracle of God.
You, too, are somebody.

the miracle of me
chapter 1

I'm — I'm what, Lord?
I'm somebody?
Well, thank you, Lord.
   That's a very nice thing
   for you to say, although I really doubt . . .

Oh, I'm sorry; I didn't mean
   to interrupt,
   especially while you are
   saying that I'm OK.
And I'm also a — a what? Again, excuse me;
   I didn't catch that.
"A unique, unrepeatable miracle of God"?
   Wow! How about that!

But give me a little help, Lord:
   I understand each of those words
   (although "miracle" sometimes baffles me);
   however, I don't quite get
   the full meaning of that sentence.
I'm not trying to be either dense or difficult
   and I recognize that I started all this
   by asking you to tell me who I am.
But what I had in mind, if you please,
   were words like "good" and "deserving"
   — that is, if you feel the truth
   can be bent just a trifle.
This "unique, unrepeatable miracle" bit
   seems way out.
   (No pun intended, Lord.)
Would you please draw a picture
   that even I can understand?

Yes, I know the meaning of "unique."
   It means "something than which there's no other"
   — or something like that.
   "One of a kind," really, although I fear
   that "unique" has been robbed
   of its meaning through overuse.

But, Lord, am I really all that different?
   I mean, my head bone is connected

to my neck bone;
My neck bone is connected
to my shoulder bone
— and on and on, don't you know.
Nothing very different
from a billion or so other men.
I'm really very ordinary
    except for my belly
    which puts me way ahead.
Yessir, I myself thought this remark
    rather clever,
    although I'll admit I doubted whether
    I should be that familiar with you.
I can still hear my saintly mother
and my boyhood pastor
shushing me for that kind of remark.
So, thank you for being
    so good-humored with me;
    I know it's difficult at times.
I really do like you
    just as you are,
    and I'm glad that you
    are taking a liking to me
    just as I am, too.

My Bible-centered mother used to remind me:
    "There's a time and a place for all things:
    A time to dance, a time to . . ."
    Oh, I forget!
I myself have to agree
    that when one begins to talk
    about his mind, body, and spirit,
    it's time to get real serious.
Because, Lord, as you well know,
    I've been hunting for an answer
    to that burning question

"Who am I?"
a powerfully long time.
(Forty years, in fact.)

Let me retrace my journey, Lord,
    although you know it as well as I.
I'd like to go back over it
    on the outside chance
    that I missed some clues
    right under my feet.

In my youth, you'll remember,
    I committed my life to you,
    although I wasn't quite sure
    just what that meant.
But even beyond this, I pledged myself
    to the "full-time ministry."
Translated, this meant:
    seminary and graduate school,
    years of teaching and preaching,
    building a church, and mending fences.
During this period, I minded
    my p's and q's —
    "performance" and "progress,"
    "quid pro quo" and "quadrennium";
    not to mention my b's —
    the banker and the bishop.
Still, the ecclesiastical ladder
    didn't deliver me into my personhood.

Yes, Lord, it's true
    that I've done too much talking
    and not enough listening.
I hear you saying
    that I've spent too much time

grabbling for the roots of life's meanings
in the unproductive soils of the past.
You say that the past is a place
for history to live, not people!
That I should accept my past,
even appropriate it, and then move on.

But, Lord, that isn't quite fair,
because I've also sought my identity
in the present.
I've designed programs, built an institution,
and tried to emulate
the Spiritual Giants of my day.

And, I've looked to the future, too, Lord.
I've taken you at your word
about rewards by and by:
mansions in the sky,
meeting face to face,
and things like that.

But although I've explored the realms
of Past, Present, and Future,
I still haven't discovered the answer
to the riddle called "me."

Enough of your prattle!
Be still and know that I am God.
Where you've failed to look
is in realities:
the realities of here and now,
open trust, and freed-up love;
the realities of your sonship,
your capacity for relationships.
In short, your personhood!

Express your uniqueness!
Ask yourself:
   "If I don't do it, then who will?
   If I don't do it now,
   when will it be done?
   For this moment is fleeting
   and will never again pass this way
   — nor will I!"

Yes, you are a miracle
   (which is a miracle in itself).
   And what is even stranger:
   all of this is a gift,
   given with no strings attached.
Forget about proving your worth;
   it was proved 2,000 years ago
   by one who demonstrated
   that faith is to be lived
   and life celebrated.
You do not have to grovel,
   nor puff yourself up.
What can you gain by all your probing,
   weighing, measuring, comparing,
   stretching, and straining?
In one brief peak moment, I can lift you
   to heights you couldn't possibly climb
   and lend you vision clearer than any eyes.

Live inside out, not outside in
   — know yourself, be yourself, express yourself
   both when you're alone and in a community.
All you really have to do
   is to be
   and express
   the authentic you!

So, celebrate!

what's in my pot?
chapter 2

In my childhood, I eagerly watched for two events to roll around: Christmas and the county fair. The fair meant taking hair-raising rides, eating cotton candy, watching games of chance, and sneaking a look at the ladies who resembled the women in the Sears Roebuck catalog.

The swings, whip, and tiltawhirl all took my breath, but their unnerving didn't last. Not so the Hall of Mirrors.

You remember. You stood in front of one mirror and it blew you up like an overstuffed elephant. But then you stepped before another mirror and instantly you were shrunk to the size of a puppy dog. Worst of all was the crazy mirror, which twisted you so that your arms came out your ears.

I'd stand in front of these mirrors and wonder, "Is this really *me*?" Indeed, before the crazy mirror, I'd check to see that it wasn't reflecting someone else nearby. Once home, I'd go into my mother's bedroom and stand in front of her full-length mirror and relish the reassurance that I still was me.

I've been alternately frightened and calmed by mirror effects most of my life. Only recently have I been able to free myself from an image-dominated style of living.

Most of my time was spent in front of the diminishing mirror — the mirror of *low self-worth*. I viewed myself as unappreciated, even worthless. This image filled me with anxiety, frustration, and unrecognized anger.

Having been crushed by this mirror, I quickly rushed over to the magnifying mirror — the mirror of *performance*. Now I appeared big and important. Having minimized my limitations, my success was assured.

The magnifying effect did not last, however. A momentary glance back into the diminishing mirror and all the air hissed out of me, leaving me deflated, small, and lifeless once again.

Then followed the crazy mirror of *futility*. It pictured me as being mixed up beyond repair. I was a hopeless nobody.

The tragedy of this mirror business was that none of these mirrors ever told me who I *really* was, for a mirror is merely a projection, lacking depth and meaning.

This book is the story of my journey to discover the *real* me. It is a story of progress and hope, and a growing recognition that failures of performance and instances of rebuff need not be disastrous; indeed, they can be utilized.

A friend from Chicago pinpointed a valid insight when he said to me, "If we Christians began to experience and appreciate our uniqueness, what a difference it would make!"

"It surely would," I responded. "We would become real — confident — able to think, feel, and act positively and constructively."

"Try this affirmation," my friend suggested. *"I am a unique, unrepeatable miracle of God."*

"Wow! That really grabs me!"

As implausible as it may sound, my friend's picture of me is true. I *am* a unique, unrepeatable miracle of God, and so are you. I am unique biologically, psychologically, rationally, and existentially. And I am unrepeatable, for there will never be another me. I am also a miracle, as are all of God's creations. But the question is, "Can I permit myself to be this kind of a being?" Can I accept my acceptance — that is, can I accept myself as God accepts me? The answer is, I'm trying. I'm living my life out of the certainty that I have worth, and as a result, I'm joyful, confident, and vastly more effective.

Think with me for a moment. What holds you and me back more than anything else? *Ourselves.* Not our *real* selves, but false selves who are unable or unwilling to see us as unique miracles of God and reservoirs of infinite value.

Nowadays, I usually feel warmly aware that things inside me are right and that I am right with God and the world. However, there are occasions when my confidence is shaken. In these times my old doubts about myself creep out of the dark corners where I have chased them, and they gnaw away at the foundations of my being just as a vast colony of termites consumes the sills of a house.

I'm trying to give you a picture of my struggle to maintain my sense of self-worth. I desperately want to reveal myself to you — but how can anyone tell another person what he feels in his gut?

Maybe a pictorial device which Virginia Satir used during a conference sponsored by Georgia State University in Atlanta will help.[1] Virginia described a huge, black pot back on the Wisconsin farm where she was reared. This pot served a multiplicity of purposes. When hogs were butchered, the pot was used for cooking out fat, and later it was used for making soap out of this same fat. During the harvest, the pot was used for cooking stew for a crowd of hungry workers. In the winter, the pot was used to mulch fertilizer for spring flowers. This pot, then, was an essential implement.

The two questions most frequently asked about the pot were:

1. "What's in the pot?"
2. "How full is the pot?"

Virginia applied the pot idea to feelings of self-worth. "Full pot" means I'm feeling good about myself — I'm on top of my situation. "Low pot," on the other hand, means I'm feeling worthless — my situation is on top of me. (There are, of course, many degrees in between.)

Let me ask you those two questions:

"What's in your pot?" Are you feeling good about yourself? On top of things? Or, are you feeling low?

"How full is your pot?" Is it bubbling to the brim and spilling over? Or, is it getting dry?

How do you answer?

Everyone covets a full pot, and becoming a Christian is one step toward acquiring a full pot. But there's a hitch. Many sincere Christians assume that once a full pot, always a full pot. And many well-meaning teachers present Christian commitment as a *permanent cure* for low self-worth. They imply that once we come into a relationship with Christ and feel him touch the core of our being, we are forever freed from feelings of worthlessness.

"When you have placed your life in God's hands, you need have no concern for either your past or your future," these persons say. "When you know God loves you, you will automatically like yourself," they imply.

Reliance upon personal commitment alone as a panacea for low self-worth can be futile. It was for me. As a youth, I had a conversion experience. Thereafter, I felt that if I could sufficiently deepen my commitment to Christ, all my feelings of "low pot" would be replaced with buoyancy and fullness. It didn't work.

Perhaps you, too, have had this expectation and have subsequently suffered a letdown. Let's say you attend a conference and hear an inspiring speaker who leads you to a deeper commitment to Jesus Christ.

Or, a friend speaks to you about your relationship to Christ and helps you to discover God's plan for your life. Or, a Lay Witness Mission in your church fills you with joy as a dozen visiting lay persons share with you how Christ has reached into their lives.

During and following such a mountaintop experience, a sense of being accepted by Christ fills your mind and spirit. Suppose that immediately after such an experience, I ask you, "What's in your pot?"

"I have love and joy in my pot. I feel accepted by God and I feel loving toward all persons. My life has real significance."

"Then your pot is full?" I inquire.

"Oh, yes, wonderfully full."

Understand, I'm not knocking peak experiences. I affirm both their validity and their importance. Peak encounters with God provide us with clues to our identity and our destiny, and to rub souls with vibrant Christians makes our pots bubble. The trouble is that we expect God, because of our oath of allegiance, to keep us on the spiritual welfare rolls for the rest of our lives. We want to sit back and let God do all the work, but a passive role won't succeed. Instead, we have to participate in our personal growth. We have to change our self-image, alter our patterns of reacting, and take charge of our automatic defenses.

Let me review some of the frustrations that grew out of my false reliance upon peak experiences. (I'd like to use the present tense, as it best captures my moods.)

I have made a new commitment to God through my association with a prayer group. I have arrived at a high level of spiritual awareness; moreover, I'm confident that this newly found buoyancy will continue indefinitely. *This time, for sure, I've got those old, negative feelings expelled.*

A few weeks pass. Strange, but that face in the mirror isn't beaming as it was a few days ago. What's wrong? Are my old attitudes coming back? I try unsuccessfully to ignore symptoms of a relapse. Soon, loneliness, guilt, and depression sweep over me.

Only a short while ago, God delivered me from these same feelings. Being a sincere Christian, I am confident that he will deliver me again. Still, what about the vision I had during my first peak experience? Was it real? Well, if it was fantasy, then I prefer to live in the wonderful world of make-believe rather than go back to the painful world of reality.

I convince myself that the ecstatic experience itself was valid, but I conclude that in the interim period I have somehow displeased God. I recall several possible infractions, and although I cannot point to any one of them as the specific reason for my low self-worth, I persuade myself that I ought to feel guilty — and soon I *am* feeling guilty. My contrition affords me relief and I conjecture that I ought to feel penitent all the time. But soon my posture of guilt grows tiring and I feel worse than ever.

Hesitantly, I reveal my doubts about myself and my spiritual life to a sharing group whom I'm learning to trust. I expect understanding — and a solution. On the contrary, their responses are negative and confusing. I come away suspecting that they, too, are hooked on bad feelings about themselves.

With my pot barren, I question the thoroughness of my confession, the honesty of my commitment, the sincerity of my motivation. I read again the Bible passages which earlier gave me a lift; I pray harder and longer. Nothing helps.

Finally, I conclude that my faith needs an "adjustment," as a chiropractor might adjust the bones of the spinal column. A prominent clergyman is to lead a retreat the following weekend. Maybe that retreat is just what I need.

The persuasive platform speaker and the community of dedicated Christians at that retreat reassure me that I have value. I come away believing that once again I have found the cure. My pot is gloriously full. Following that, I do not let problems encountered in my daily routine throw a shadow upon my relationship with God. I do not panic. I merely seek out another peak experience with other good Christians. Each outing helps, but it doesn't afford lasting relief.

I don't recognize it, but I'm riding a sinister merry-go-round. I ride the horse of piety and personal discipline; then

I ride the horse of small-group sharing; next I ride the lay witness horse, and then the retreat horse. The horses go up and down, round and round, but I'm getting nowhere. Sadly, my frantic quest for fulfillment is addictive. I cannot get off the merry-go-round. Evenings and weekends, I'm dashing somewhere seeking someone who can reaffirm my commitment, stoke my zeal, coach me in Christian enthusiasm.

When I have ridden the merry-go-round a hundred times, the real me begins hammering at the door of my consciousness. I pause and take a bearing. I see that I haven't progressed, but have been traveling in circles.

I call this madcap pursuit of spiritual well-being the "commitment syndrome." It is a frenzied chase *"out there"* for *inner* peace. It has its own self-destruct button.

Bored, fatigued, and frustrated, I begin searching for a better way. If God really loves me and wills for me to know his love, then I want to *accept* his love instead of forever *pursuing* it. I want to *live* my Christian life instead of continually *fondling* it.

Now I recognize that my pot of self-worth was created from good materials by a master craftsman, God himself. It isn't the pot that's to blame — rather, the blame lies with me for letting its contents grow sour. And the contents of the pot are most likely to sour when I'm trying to find myself outside myself.

For twenty years my pot was sour, but I didn't want to acknowledge it. When I recognized there was trouble in my pot, I hoped that time would cure it, but it didn't. Then, a bit later, I went from one peak experience to another gathering pepper and parsley to toss into the pot, but neither the spice nor the garnish was of lasting help. Only after a great deal of deep and honest reflection, study, and prayer did I see the truth: I would have to get that contamination out of my pot and keep it out.

I've been working hard to understand who I am and why. Why I have the feelings that I have. Why I react to persons and situations as I do. I've tried to inventory both my assets and my limitations. Acquiring self-understanding hasn't been easy. And the second step, living out of my discoveries, has been even more difficult for me to do.

Considering the point from which I started, I think that I've made good progress toward reorienting my life. I still have a long way to go, and occasionally I slip. I've also fallen victim to detours, dead ends, and *culs de sac*. I think the term *cul de sac* is especially appropriate here because it means a blind alley or blocked corridor which was designed that way. The little circles at the end of one-way streets are *culs de sac* — they're there to facilitate your coming out the same way you went in.

Many of the streets that I took in my search for spiritual renewal were *culs de sac*. Let me describe several of them:

Utopia Street. I entered this street the first day I became a Christian. I thought it led to spiritual perfection. After twenty years of frequenting this street, I discovered that it lived up to its name. "Utopia" means *not a place*. For a Christ-person, there is no place that is a utopia. There is only the real world.

Methodology Street. While on this street, I practiced the methodology used by the saints. This was helpful, but I became so bound by methods that I was blocked from experiencing the free flowing of the Spirit of God. And the more structured I became, the more I fenced out awareness of God's immediate presence.

Castle Street. On this street, I found a castle into which I retreated. Ensconced there, I became more and more oblivious to the world around me and more and more encased in my latest theological concept, supremely confident that I had the truth.

When each of these routes turned out to be dead ends, I began circling a cloverleaf, hoping for a new, and sure, path to becoming somebody. After a while, I discovered that I had to extricate myself from frozen methods, raze my spiritual castle, dismiss my longing for a spiritual utopia, and, finally, forsake the cloverleaf and head out on the main road to life. There are no short cuts.

The journey takes time, risk, and pain. I have to understand who I am, decide upon a direction, and move out!

Now that I face life more directly, I feel better about myself and about other people. My relationships with God and my associates are richer. I function better. Life makes sense. And embracing reality hasn't robbed me of ecstasy at all. I still have peak experiences. I just do not expect them to contribute more than they are capable of contributing to my life.

I believe that God created me for a purpose, a very special purpose. I do not have a precise and complete picture of what that purpose is. Instead, God reveals my vocation to me bit by bit, hour by hour, day by day. Usually, his purpose unfolds in the matrix of daily living rather than when I'm immersed in solitude and reflection.

At times I don't know quite what to do about some of my worst traits — such as my emotional immaturity. At times I'm dismayed by my physical self — for example, my being much larger than average size. At times hurts from the past, including wasted opportunities, plague me. However, I have matured sufficiently to push aside the temptation to wallow in self-pity and to look for easy ways out; I have learned to buckle down to authentic living, accepting my limitations along with my strong points and using both constructively.

Nobody is blessed with a pot that's eternally full, always sweet, forever bubbling. Everyone experiences low pot and sour pot from time to time.

In this chapter, I've tried to share with you how it's been with me in my quest for wholeness. In the chapters which follow, I will further describe my journey. I hope you'll come along and that you will occasionally find an insight that you can apply to advantage in your own search for fulfillment.

the ok gospel
chapter 3

Have you ever seen a computer in operation? I hadn't until a friend took me on a tour of the IBM offices in Atlanta and described a project that was in progress. I won't be too technical here (in fact, I didn't understand all that I saw), but let me give you a thumbnail description.

My host showed me printed forms on which the employees of a corporation had entered personal data — age, address, marital status, etc. A woman was punching this information into cards, each bit of data becoming a distinctively placed perforation.

"Let's say that you want to prepare your older employees for retirement," my friend said. He placed a batch of the punched cards into a "sorter." As the motor whirred, the cards zipped through the machine and out into compartments.

My friend took the cards from one compartment. "Here we have the cards of all employees who are between ages sixty and sixty-five," he said. "We could even separate out those who play golf."

My host showed me how the information on the cards was transferred onto magnetic tape and stored in the computer. At a keyboard, he typed out a request for the names of all employees who had expressed an interest in management training — data which had already been processed.

As I watched the machine type out those names, I recognized that the computer and I have much in common. I, too, contain "magnetic tapes." All my life experiences are on file in my "computer."

When somebody "types on my keyboard," I respond. If he says "beach," I recall pleasant, sun-filled days spent at the ocean's edge. But if he types "preacher," I respond with feelings of isolation and loneliness, because I do not want to be known by a title — I want to be recognized as a person.

Of course, my psychological processes are vastly more complicated than the workings of a computer. Still, I'm programmed, and when people around me either criticize or commend me, I respond out of stored experiences and feelings. My response is joyous or sad, confident or fearful. Sometimes, before I can react constructively, a destructive pattern of responding which is stored in my computer takes charge.

Although I am *like* a computer, I am *not* a computer! I am a human being. I can choose to change. Unlike the computer, which is limited to parroting back data just as it was recorded, I can interpret. I can either accept my computer's print-out or I can say, "That's how I *was*, but I will not be like that any more." I call my tendency to resign myself to old patterns of responding the "computer trap." It's as deadly as the "commitment syndrome."

To break out of the computer trap, I need to understand how I function. How did I come to have the data that is stored within me? Why do I respond as I do when somebody types on my keyboard? How can I take charge of these responses?

Like a computer operator, I need a manual which gives me a clear understanding of how my computer works. Not *all* the answers, but simply a way of getting at my feelings and reactions. Such a manual is *I'm OK — You're OK*, written by Thomas Harris, a psychiatrist.[2] Although, in my opinion, the book has flaws and blind spots, it is quite helpful.

Dr. Harris describes four basic attitudes toward life. He calls these the "four life positions." They are:

1. I'm not OK — you're OK.
2. I'm not OK — you're not OK.
3. I'm OK — you're not OK.
4. I'm OK — you're OK.

All children, being small and helpless, begin life with a stance of "You're OK but I'm not OK." From birth to age five, the child interprets his situation in terms of "I don't understand all of what's going on around here, but I can see that these giant people are powerful and seem to know everything. I'd better try to please them because I'm dependent upon them to meet my needs."

Having this perspective, the child spends a great deal of his time asking himself, "How can I act so that these OK people will tell me that I, too, am OK?" Consequently, the child develops patterns of thinking and acting which invoke approval, or "stroking," as Harris puts it. Some of this childlike dependency persists in adulthood — more so in some persons than in others.

The second life position, "I'm not OK — you're not OK," is typical of the person who, in his second or third year, failed to receive stroking. Such a child concludes that his needs aren't going to be met, so why subject himself to the pain of seeking fulfillment? An extreme expression of this stance is hopelessness and total withdrawal — and, eventually, institutionalization or suicide.

The third life position, "I'm OK — you're not OK," has criminal implications. This stance is characterized by the battered (physically abused) child. This person finds his environment unfriendly. As he nurses his hurts, he "strokes" himself. He builds himself a protective shell from which he lashes out at the world.

The fourth position, "I'm OK, you're OK," is the mature stance. It permits mutuality and trust. Importantly, it is elective.

We tend to carry over into adulthood the attitude that we developed during our formative childhood years. We characterize ourselves and are characterized by whichever of these four life stances predominates. Understand, we're talking of our *predominant* life position. Our responses may vary with a given challenge. Even the neurotic person feels OK some of the time. The question is whether we see ourselves as *basically* OK or not OK.

As I read Harris' book, I became painfully aware that I have lived most of my life from a *not*-OK stance. I had sensed this all along — Harris merely presented me with a handy way to identify and classify my attitudes. I began life, as everyone does, in an "I'm not OK" position. Unfortunately, I have been too long growing out of that stance.

When, as a teen-ager, I was converted to Jesus Christ, I brought along a great deal of insecurity and guilt. For perhaps six months, the sense of God's forgiveness gave me deep personal release. Then my pot began to sour. My alarm and despair led me to the commitment syndrome which I described in Chapter 1. For two decades, I reasoned that if committing my life to Christ had given me release, then a still deeper commitment would produce even greater release. This pursuit of personal piety as a source for identity proved unproductive because, in my blindness, I was avoiding basic internal changes.

19

Harris helped me realize that my life-filter (my predominant life-stance) had to be changed. I was handicapped by a *not-OK* filter. As long as my life experiences poured through this not-OK filter, they would be contaminated. Until I changed my perception of myself and all of my life experiences, I would continue to feel impoverished no matter how often I recommitted myself to God. Seeing that self-condemnation served no good purpose, I determined to rid my life of contaminating influences and to replace my not-OK filter with an OK filter.

What Harris calls "not-OK feelings," the theologians have labeled "original sin." Not-OK feelings grow out of and are intensified by the child's anxiety about his physical survival, his hunger for emotional stroking, and his fear of rejection by his parents and parent-figures. The child begins life with this burden of insecurity. Similarly, the doctrine of original sin presupposes that man is burdened with anxiety simply because he is born human. When this doctrine is distorted to imply that man is born evil, the distortion can evoke self-rejection and contempt for one's humanness.

Harris does not elaborate his idea in theological terms, although he does say that taking the OK position is akin to a religious conversion. I would like to raise a flag of warning. Neither declaring an OK position (in humanistic terms) nor a conversion (in conventional religious terms) provides permanent "all-right" feelings. I agree that you have to reconstruct your self-image and overhaul your patterns of response, but my experience indicates that a declaration of "I'm OK — you're OK" is sheer mental gymnastics unless this affirmation is based upon and bulwarked by the grace of God. My sense of OK-ness must have roots which provide substance and durability, else I'm floating on a cloud of illusion. The necessary holding power is the Christian message that I am OK in spite of my weaknesses, failures, and sins. God revealed this in the life, teachings, death, and resurrection of Jesus.

For this realization merely to break into my mind isn't enough, however. I must *live out of* a sense of my OK-ness. This entails reprogramming both my perceptions and responses.

After reading Harris' book, I came to see the Gospel of Christ as the Gospel of OK. Christ says to me, "Sure, you've got all that data in your computer, some of it good, some bad, some unresolved. And, yes, you have this predominant life-stance of not-OK. But I accept you anyhow. I don't enjoy seeing you torture yourself with feelings of inadequacy. You're OK with me, so see yourself as OK and start living that way. I assure you that you can become more authentic. It won't be easy, but you can do it. And you'll be glad you did."

Lately, while listening to people, I've been sorting their remarks into OK piles and not-OK piles. See if you agree with me that an *I'm not OK, but you are* Christian expresses himself in these ways:

"Our preacher really got us told in his sermon today!"

"Preacher, I wish I had the source of power that you do."

"My church means so much to me, but I can never live up to the standards that it holds up before me."

"I wish I could live the kind of Christian life that I see in Catherine Marshall."

"I feel small and insignificant, but God is great and powerful. He could never concern himself with me."

These statements arise from a not-OK life position.

"The minister — the church — other Christians — God — they're all OK, but I'm not."

Do you often feel little (not-OK) when you compare yourself with others? Do you attempt to buy the approval of significant persons by depreciating yourself? It's fine to appreciate others, but self-depreciation is destructive.

Now, look at some typical expressions of Christians who feel that *"I'm not OK, but neither are you"*:

"I admit I'm not the Christian I ought to be, but if that preacher's attitude is Christian, I don't want any part of it."

"I'm not so hot as a citizen, but the church has no business getting involved in social issues like race."

"I can't believe there's a God, because if there were, he wouldn't have put me in the lousy situation I'm in."

These persons are saying, "I'm not OK and neither is anyone else. I don't like myself and I don't like others."

Harris says that the third life-stance, *"I'm OK, but you aren't,"* predisposes a criminal mentality. Without being that harsh, let me repeat some expressions that I've heard within "Christian" communities:

"When I met God, I received the truth, so I know that those who differ from me are lost."

"Unless you get religion like I did, you ain't got nothing."

"You may call yourself a Christian, but unless you interpret the word of God as I do, you're deluding yourself."

"If you were truly Christian, you would see that my church is the right one."

When my understanding of God becomes absolute and ultimate authority, any contradiction produces a painful conflict for me. Such a conflict can be pursued to this end: "If he's right, I'm wrong. If I'm wrong about my faith, I'm lost, and I can't bear to think about that." So, instead of facing the issues which give rise to my feeling of doubt and inadequacy, I retreat to my absolute position and picture myself invulnerable. "I'm OK, but you're not."

Differentness can be threatening, true, so the tendency to pull back is understandable. But if my insecurity proceeds to the point where I reject the other person, shut out all new ideas, and retreat into isolation, my conduct is neither theologically correct nor socially acceptable. I will become bankrupt. If I am to be OK, I must accept my OK-ness as a gift. I cannot receive it on the basis that I think, feel, or act in a manner superior to you. Such a stance contradicts the good news of Christ.

The fourth life-position, *"I'm OK and you're OK,"* is a mature and Christian stance, permitting expressions like these:

"I appreciated the honesty of our minister in sharing his own struggles. Now I see him as a real person like me."

"Although my church is not an infallible guide to conduct, it is made up of persons who are trying to become what God intended us to be."

"I have a friend who betrayed our relationship, but maybe he was dealing with something within himself that I don't understand just now."

22

"I have begun to love and accept myself because God loves me."

If it is true that you are a *unique, unrepeatable miracle of God*, then you are responsible for discovering your OK self and expressing yourself in an OK way. The fourth life-position is the only position which permits you to fulfill your destiny. The first position makes *you* not OK. The second makes *everybody* not OK. The third stance makes you OK while *everyone else* is not OK. Only in the fourth position are you and other persons OK. This stance alone supports a positive self-image and nurtures constructive relationships. Isn't this the basis for the admonition to love God with your whole heart and your neighbor as yourself? And is this not living in the grace of God?

In contrast, let's look at the Not-OK Gospel. This gospel begins with Adam. God created Adam as a unique, unrepeatable miracle. (So far, so good.) But just as we moderns do, Adam sought to fulfill his being in ways that contradicted his true nature. As a result, Adam felt uncomfortable, and to deal with his anxiety, he made a garment of leaves. (Just as you and I develop our cover-ups when we feel estranged.) Out of his insecure feelings, Adam assumed that God had wiped him out, written him off, as punishment for his failure.

Let's pause for a moment and consider the implications of this assumption. Today, many persons assume that they, being human, were born under this curse. This, then, is the Not-OK Gospel. We would be stuck with this gospel if God had not provided us a better understanding of his purposes. Christ incarnated the OK Gospel. The Bible is a story of God's revealing himself to men, and the disclosure becomes complete in Jesus Christ. In Christ, God came in the flesh and lived among us. By participating in our humanity, God said, "It's OK to be a human being; it's even OK to have a full range of human drives. After all, I created you like that."

In retrospect, it becomes apparent that God continued to relate to Adam. God gave Adam a task. Along with the task came instructions which would permit Adam to become the person that God intended. Adam was accepted by God.

Adam's difficulty was his refusal to accept his acceptance. By exercising trust and obedience, Adam could have turned his bad news into good news; instead, he let not-OK feelings defeat him.

Christ modeled the I'm OK — you're OK style. Jesus didn't depend upon external sanctions. For example, when he was accused of being a winebibber, a gluttonous man, a friend of publicans and sinners, a transgressor of the Sabbath laws, Christ did not feel undone; he continued to devote himself to the highest principle of life, which is to love God with one's whole being and to love one's neighbor as one's self. Christ continued to live out of a sense of his real identity, and his pot of self-worth was filled by the unending stream of God's love. Christ's OK-ness permitted him to accept death on the cross, and his resurrection assures us that we can conquer our own feelings of futility.

Having been given Christ's example of an OK life-style, why has mankind through 2,000 years continued to live out of a gospel of *not* OK? Why has man spun his wheels devising one political, social, and religious system after another, each complete with its own rules and regulations? This question is interesting, but academic when compared with the question, "Why do *you* and *I* continue to live out of a not-OK position when we know this isn't God's intention?"

I have a free choice of life-styles. If I choose, I can live according to the Not-OK Gospel, which asserts that God had a good idea when he created the world — the only trouble is, it just doesn't work. Man is inherently bad; therefore, I am bad. My true expression of myself is sin. Obviously, to choose the Not-OK Gospel has painful consequences.

Or, I can live according to the OK Gospel: God created me a unique person of worth; in Christ, he has accepted me just as I am. He has given me unlimited potential for being his person in his world.

I don't know about you, but I have found that I cannot find fulfillment by adopting standards outside myself. I cannot measure myself by somebody else's set of rules, or by some significant person, or even a noble institution. At one time I needed a "parent" to reassure me that I was OK, but that time is past. I cannot continue in spiritual childhood; I have to become a *man* (and you a woman, if you're of the other sex). I have to quit trying to delegate my responsibility to be myself. I'm OK — and you're OK — because God says so.

I'll never wipe out all the negative data on the tapes within me. This data will replay from time to time. I must acknowledge my stored not-OK information and impressions, but I can refuse to let them *control* my life.

If God is for you, who or what can be against you? And if God is for you, why should you be against yourself? Embrace your OK-ness. Celebrate it. Live in the glow of the self-worth which the OK Gospel offers.

who am I plugged into?
chapter 4

One major question that I have asked myself is, "Who am I?" The answer has been a long time coming because for so many years I sought my identity in the wrong places — in persons and institutions *outside* myself: parents, teachers, peers, colleges, business and professional organizations, the church. And through the church, I petitioned a God "up there somewhere" to tell me who I was.

When I posed the question "Who am I?" to these persons and institutions, I received confusing and contradictory answers. One person would give me his version of who I was and I would concur, "Yes, that's right. That's who I am." But then someone else would paint a different picture and I would try to buy it. Sometimes I recognized that the reflected images were not right — I could feel it in my gut. The problem was, I wasn't willing to trust my gut feelings.

Now I can see that I was playing a game similar to one that I have used in group experiences.

As each person arrives, I pin on his back the name of a well-known character, either real or fictitious. His goal is to discover his assumed identity. He goes to the other members of the group and displays his name tag. In response, they give him clues to his identity through pantomime. Often their characterizations are faulty, their gestures clumsily executed. Inevitably, there are many false starts and false guesses — which is fun *for a game*.

In my deadly serious "Who Am I?" game, I was going around asking outside sources this question, and I was getting a lot of misleading clues.

In his *I'm OK — You're OK*, Harris explains that I was clinging to my childlike, inferior, dependent position. I wasn't OK, so I was incapable of knowing who I was. But I reasoned that these other people, being OK, ought to know. So when they attempted to tell me who I was, their voices rang with authority. Mother, teacher, preacher, peer group — these people spoke to me out of roles of omniscient, omnipotent parents.

As with most children, my primary relationship was with my mother. During my gestation, all of my nourishment flowed from my mother to me through an umbilical cord. The severing of this cord shortly after my birth represented a first step toward my becoming independent. But no sooner had the physical cord been snipped than a psychic cord took its place. I then plugged this psychic cord into my mother — and I did this for many years, especially during times of emotional stress. I felt that if I lost my relationship with my mother, I would cease to be.

Certainly until about age six, my mother was the most significant person in my life. Fortunately, she was a good mother. She loved me dearly and she demonstrated her love. She was so good and so loving that I could not bear the thought of hurting her. She aspired for me to be a good boy and to amount to something. I felt that if I failed to live up to her expectations, I would cause her tremendous hurt, and she might reject me. My mother strained to reassure me that her love was not dependent upon my performance, but somehow I could not accept this message. If I failed, she might reject me. I was in the untenable situation of attempting to achieve positive goals out of a negative motivation.

It's perfectly natural (and desirable) for a child to have a close relationship with his or her mother. And it is through the mother that the child gets his first directions for life. But there must come a time when the child begins to shift toward his own set of priorities. In this respect, my development was retarded. My state of dependency continued into my adulthood. I desperately needed approval, and as additional persons became significant to me, I began asking them, "Who am I?" Again and again, their answers seemed to imply that my identity was to be found in their approval. I began asking myself, "What does this significant person expect of me?" My reasoning was that if I could find out what he wanted me to be, I could be it. If I could perform up to his expectations, he would say, "You're OK."

A performance orientation is hazardous and, in the end, fatal. Your performance may not please the other person. If he is critical, his negative response confirms your own estimate of yourself as a not-OK person. "I knew I couldn't do it, and his criticism proves it." And even if the person with a low self-image wins approval, he is incapable of accepting the compliment as deserved and well-intended. Instead, he rationalizes: "That guy wouldn't know a good performance if he saw one." Or, "Well, I fooled him this time, but I know I didn't do well and eventually he will see it too."

Often, I found myself doubting the sincerity of expressions of appreciation. For example, I didn't like history and considered myself a poor history student. There was, however, a teacher whose approval I coveted, so for a while I studied hard. One day, she called on me and I gave her a good answer, whereupon she stated to the class that I was one of her best students. After class, I began to doubt the sincerity of her remark: *I hate history and I'm not good at it. She's trying to butter me up. She's trying to trick me into studying harder.* Soon, I had rejected her compliment.

This may seem an innocent little misadventure, but it wasn't. It reflects a pattern which became a part of my personality. I adopted a method of systematically rejecting most favorable responses. *I don't like me, so why should anyone else like me? I'm not capable or competent, so why should anyone say that I am?* Indeed, when I entered into a Christian commitment, I viewed it my duty to set the record straight and disavow undeserved praise. So, I was between a rock and a hard place. If I didn't draw favorable responses, I felt rejected; yet, if I was commended, I felt guilty.

Rebuke or withheld praise were especially devastating when they confirmed my impressions of myself. For example, the high school football coach was one of my idols. In my junior year, I was out of shape and loafing during practices. One day, the coach ordered me to take extra laps around the field. I did, but in a shirking manner.

"Johnson," the coach said, "turn in your uniform. If you aren't going to put more effort into football than you've displayed today, I don't have time to fool with you."

His rejection shattered me; I felt completely exposed. He confirmed what I had often told myself, "You're a poor player. You don't block well. And you don't hold onto the ball on a pass because you know somebody is going to slam into you if you do." In effect, I had asked the coach, "Am I as lousy a player as I think I am?" and he had replied, "Yes!" But I couldn't tolerate the answer.

Later that afternoon, the coach came into the locker room and said he was going to give me another chance. This was a compliment, but I couldn't relish it; his rebuke seemed more valid.

No adult mattered so much to me as did my peer group. I lived in the country, about seven miles from town. My city cousins liked to visit me. We played cowboy, rode horses and steers, and had a good time generally. But I dreaded going into town to visit them because they often introduced me as their "little country cousin." I'm sure they intended no insult, but their introduction made me feel inferior. Their words confirmed my own low estimate of myself.

Earlier, I mentioned replacing my physical umbilical cord with a psychic umbilical cord, a new connection which I first plugged into my mother. Continuing my search for self-identity, I plugged this psychic cord into my teachers, coach, and peers. Still later, I plugged into four mother-surrogates. These mother-figures were (1) God (a God "out there"), (2) college and academics, (3) my wife, and (4) my job.

I was a teen-ager when I plugged into a relationship with God. It was a one-sided relationship. I was not OK, while God was the ultimate of OK-ness. I could only ask him to forgive me for my weakness. I promised that if he would give me another chance, I would do better. Again, *performance*.

I set out to "please" God. But first, I had to ascertain what he wanted me to do; more importantly, what did he *not* want me to do? When I sought answers to these questions, I got a lot of bad help. There were many eager souls who, featuring themselves as God's spokesman, glibly spouted out lists of do's and don'ts — especially don'ts. As a result, I got a very shallow picture of God's love for me. Loaded with good intention and poor advice, I set out on a please-God performance binge.

After pursuing this course vigorously for a few years, I began to feel unreal. I was like a diver in a steel suit. Inside my "Christian" apparatus, I seemed to be alive, but it was so much like a coffin that I feared I was dead. I waddled around asking "Who am I?" I looked pleadingly out the glass port of my helmet, but I found myself shut off from persons around me. Besides, this costume just didn't fit my personality. I was like David in Saul's armor.

Repeatedly, my relationship with God was fractured by my feelings of unworthiness and rejection. I had developed such a strong image of worthlessness that I had difficulty accepting God's acceptance of me. Instead of being open to God's communications, I listened to my own negative feelings about myself and presumed that God was talking.

Another mother-substitute was my academic experience. I had always regarded intelligent and educated persons as *somebody*, and if anyone wanted to be somebody, it was Ben Johnson. My first quarter, I studied every spare moment. I found first-year Greek frighteningly difficult, and the vocabulary in introductory psychology was Greek to me, too. Yet, I was determined to conquer these subjects and the others. When the first quarter ended, I had four A's on the report that was mailed home to my parents.

Now I had found the route to my identity. Academic achievement would produce meaning for my life! For six consecutive quarters, I made nothing but A's. I relished the recognition, but inside I knew that this was not my true identity. I was not an academician.

I had three quarters to go when I got married. I unplugged the psychic umbilical cord from college and plugged it into my wife. Innocently but mistakenly, I assumed that this woman could be a substitute for my mother. She would provide me with the love and acceptance that I desperately needed. When I found that I could not impose the *mother* template upon the *man-wife* relationship, I suffered pain and frustration. If I only tried harder! I thereupon aspired to a superb performance as a husband, believing that this would give me my identity. This effort, too, left me with a tragic sense of having failed to achieve a sense of personhood.

I turned to a fourth parent-figure. I plugged my psychic umbilical cord into my work. I didn't disconnect from my marriage — I was still struggling there, but I began trying to ease my sense of failure as a husband by investing inordinate amounts of time and energy into being a pastor. Surely, Mother Church would tell me that I was OK — that is, *if* I performed well and thereby won her approval.

In order to become *somebody*, I fell into the trap that Phil

Barnhart calls "the Stepladder Syndrome."[3] If I could please my congregation, my district superintendent, and my bishop, these important people would say, "You're OK, move up the ladder." I performed well. I doubled the membership, the attendance, the budget, and the building. (I also doubled the indebtedness.) Still, praise from my overseers did not reward me sufficiently. For one reason or another, I rejected commendations. Again, performance had failed to produce identity.

Upon leaving the local pastorate to establish the Lay Witness Mission movement and to found the Institute of Church Renewal, I entered into a period of even more feverish activity. I spoke in major pulpits across the country. I addressed gatherings of several thousand persons. Denominational leaders sought my advice and support. Hundreds of friends said, "I'm with you, count on me." But all of these confirmations put together could not answer the question of "Who am I?" I had merely added another mother-substitute to my list.

Here I was, at age 40, disillusioned and frustrated. I still believed in the work in which I was engaged, but I had discovered that a person's work can never be a substitute for personhood. I saw that God had given me a mother, teachers, coach, peer group, college, wife, and job as *contexts* in which to work out my sense of identity, but I had instead looked upon these persons and institutions as *sources* of identity.

There was only one other place for me to look — *inside*. Into the person I had rejected. Into the self that I had avoided.

Inside my skin was a person. A person who was created in God's image. A person of value, a person with a destiny. My OK-ness did not come from frenzied activity which won the cheers of individuals or crowds. My OK-ness was a gift from God.

In my headlong race for performance, I had, in effect, gone off and left my self behind. I was very tired, for I had wasted much of my energy trying to drag along all those parent-figures to whom I was connected by psychic umbilical cords. I would have to seek another route, a different pace.

I do not wish to dismiss as unimportant the persons who have been close to me; they have contributed a great deal. And some of them tried desperately to show me the right track and get me off the dead-end trail. One of these, my good friend and counselor James W. Sells, said to me many times, "Ben, you really need for everyone to like you, don't you?" I stumbled around for an answer, saying something like, "Oh, not really," or "Oh, maybe so." Now I know that Dr. Sells, in his polite and constructive manner, was trying to help me to recognize my dependency.

The insight and strength for freeing myself from my psychic umbilical cords came to me dramatically during a personal growth experience. I became sharply aware that the psychic cords had become twisted about me, choking out the breath of life. I had to wean myself and stop trying to suck identity from these outside sources.

I found myself in a deep state of awareness. Symbolically, I grasped a machete and began hacking at the psychic cords binding me to other people and to institutions. I hacked . . . and I hacked . . . and I hacked. Then, to convince myself that I was completely freed, I whirled and flailed about me to cut any cords that I might have missed. With all the cords severed, a surge of strength came into me. *I have value because I am. My worth is a gift from God, a gift given without condition.*

Now when I reach for an identity handout, warning bells go off inside me. I remember that plugging into other persons can only produce a reflection — a reflection which necessarily will be incomplete and distorted, just as were those mirrors at the fair.

I remain vigilant so that those psychic umbilical cords will not grow back. Withdrawal from dependency has sometimes been painful, but I'm determined to live from the inside out.

living from
the inside out
chapter 5

For almost four decades, I sought my identity in persons, institutions, and activities. In other words, I lived from the outside in. Recently, I came to see that I cannot find my identity "out there." I have to live from the inside out.

In the last chapter, I related my quest, my frustration, and my awakening. Now I would like to share with you the story of another person's pilgrimage into authentic personhood.

A close friend said he had a concern that he'd like to discuss with me at lunch. When we had gotten settled, he said, "I have a deep sense of failure, and it sometimes overwhelms me. It is the failure to achieve personal identity."

"Tell me about it," I invited.

"In my teen years," he said, "I had the mixed drives and muddled feelings of the typical adolescent. The central question among the many questions that plagued me was the notorious one, 'Who am I?' I finally answered that question in this way: 'I am a musician.'

"I was at that time immersing myself in music. I was playing in a high school dance band. A really good weekend consisted of spending Saturday either practicing with the band or talking with professional musicians, then playing for a dance on Saturday night. Followed by more of the same on Sunday."

As he talked, I identified with him. In my own youthful fantasies, I had been a Glenn Miller or a Duke Ellington.

My friend continued, "While I was mesmerized by my passion for music, I hit one gigantic obstacle — my father. Although he didn't disapprove of my enjoying music or even my playing on weekends, he made it painfully clear that music would not be an acceptable career. He then proceeded to project what he expected, including the school that he expected me to attend. Incidentally, it was one of the best schools — of *business* — in the nation. The prospect of studying economics and accounting and then being chained to a desk frightened me.

"I verbally acknowledged my father's plans for me, but in practice, I denied them. In college, my style changed very little. I found a new group of musicians to pal around with. I directed a band and I composed and arranged music for fun and extra money. Meanwhile, because I had a good mind, I made acceptable grades. Interestingly, I developed my avocation of music to the point that it was economically more profitable during my senior year than my vocation was to be the first year following my graduation.

"Following college, two additional voices spoke against my fulfilling my dream of being a professional musician. First, my culture spoke: 'Musicians are a crummy bunch. They keep absurd hours, are often immoral, and generally are economically unproductive. Even if you should become a successful musician, you will still be a nobody.'

"The second and conclusive voice was heard soon after I went into military service. Because of a need to express my deep passion for music, I joined a musical group. But these fellows had spent years studying theory and practicing. They spoke a language I didn't understand; they performed with an excellence I didn't possess. Although they were tactful, I got their message that I did not have it. As I reflected on this message, I realized that I had gone to *business* school, not *music* school. I didn't feel that I could compete with pros. Thus died my latent dreams of someday finding personal fulfillment by being a professional musician."

My friend had experienced low pot, and no wonder. His sense of identity had been shattered. I asked him how this blow affected him.

"Intellectually, I felt confused," my friend continued. *"If I'm not a musician, who am I?*

"I began an import business from the Philippines. This meant a great deal of traveling along the Eastern seaboard. Most of my associates were eager to make money, and their expressions of this desire coincided with my father's expectations of me. So, I decided on a new identity: *I am a businessman who can make money.*

"In the military service, I came in contact with a man who had previously owned a successful consulting firm. He and I, with another associate, formed our own company. All of us were committed to making money, and for ten years we immersed ourselves in a campaign to build the company into a highly profitable corporation. During those years, I enjoyed the luxuries of 'expense-account living.' Since I now understood myself in terms of being a 'successful businessman,' I acquired the language of that culture. When attending trade association meetings, I carefully observed the other 'stud ducks' so I could improve my own style.

"Part of the 'stud-duck' image was a heightened social life. I already belonged to one country club, but I sought reinforcement by becoming a Three-Club Man. The club life consisted of an endless round of parties, playing golf with my foursome two weekday afternoons and Sunday afternoons, and traveling by chartered plane or company plane to sporting events.

"The church was an adjunct of my successful businessman image. I didn't inquire into the real meaning of the church or of churchmanship, for a serious questioning of life was not part of the businessman image. Instead, I needed to go to church occasionally so that whenever the situation demanded it, I could refer to my membership and my participation, nominal though it was."

"What about your family?" I interjected.

"You can imagine what it was like living with a corporation president. I kept my image intact, ordering my wife and kids about as I did my office employees. The net result was a series of broken relations, disappointment, and frustration."

An urgent tone came into my friend's voice. "Ben," he said, "when I arrived at my objective and saw myself as a 'successful businessman,' I began measuring that image. I started exploring the 'mansion' that went with the image, and I found room after room to be empty. One Saturday evening, during a cocktail party, I muttered, 'What am I doing here? I don't like the people. I don't like the trivial conversation. I'm in a crowd and presumably enjoying myself, yet I feel alone and depressed. I may very well be a successful *businessman*, but am I a successful *person*?' "

I reflected on my own life. For a long time, I was convinced that I was not OK, but that 'out there' was some OK person, some OK position, or some OK achievement that could make things OK for me. As I have already shared with you, I had experienced my friend's error again and again, and with the same frustration.

My friend's quizzical expression told me that he sensed I had strayed. "I'm sorry," I said. "Please go on."

"Our company decided to seek a merger with a larger company. I was designated to handle the search for the right company. This new assignment softened my feelings of unrest. I gained a renewed sense of importance as I worked with New York brokers and flew around the country talking with company presidents.

"As the merger negotiations progressed, however, I experienced a new threat. Where would I fit into the merged enterprise? Could I fit? Maybe not. I began to carve out a new identity for myself: I am a *retired successful businessman.*

"I put together the merger and received a sizable portion of stock. Now I reaffirmed my role of retired successful businessman. I saw myself investing the proceeds, meanwhile managing other investments I had made. I envisioned myself rising for a late breakfast, reading the *Wall Street Journal*, and checking the market reports. Then I would go to the club and have lunch with other retired successful businessmen. I would sit on corporate boards, and I would lend my expertise to civic committees. (Actually, I considered myself a failure in many respects, but I resisted this image.)

"Soon, my identity received another jolt. This time, the experience was not in the career area, but in the spiritual dimension.

"During several months spent recuperating from a disability, the reality of God began unfolding to me. I came to know myself in a way that I had never before known myself. I caught a glimpse of reality, and it excited and fascinated me. But my conversion experience wasn't without pain. I was challenged to get in touch with my *real* self. I faced the task of learning how to live from the life-drives within me rather than living out of an identity which I had fitted over me like a cloak.

"Now, Ben, my question to you is, *'How can I discover more fully who I am on the inside?'*"

My friend was deadly serious. As I reflected upon his situation and his question, I saw that he and I had made the same mistake, looking outside ourselves for identity. My friend had discovered, as I had, that a person cannot *assume* an identity; instead, he discovers it as he authentically expresses his being. He acts out of his God-given OK-ness. He lives from the inside out.

My friend and I had both gone through what might be called "conversion" experiences, although his was perhaps a more typically "religious" experience than mine was. Actually, both of us had undergone change (more change than we recognized) over long periods of time. But suddenly we realized that we must make radically different turns in our lives — and right away.

Because I had so recently reoriented my own life, I felt like a babe trying to lead another babe when I faced my friend's question. And on the scale of birth to maturity, I'm still a toddler. However, I have begun to walk on my own two legs, and I've begun to sense out my own direction rather than automatically heading for the outstretched arms of parent-figures.

I have experienced three stages of spiritual development. At first, I felt I ought to love God and please him by throwing myself into a strenuous devotional program and by doing the right things and resisting the wrong things. Next, I sensed that God loves me, not because I love him or perform well, but simply because he is God. Later, I recognized that if God made me and loves me, then I can afford to see myself as important and lovable. These three stages comprise a progression — "I love God," "God loves me," and "I love me." The three elements complement each other.

Even at the time of my conversion, I could accept myself as a *spiritual* being. I was reaching out to God, albeit in an immature fashion. My culturization had told me that it's "good" to be spiritual. My problem was with the *emotional* and *physical* aspects of my person, which so often seemed "bad." I couldn't picture God having any interest in my anatomy and physiology or my feelings and drives except to frown upon them now and then.

Certainly I felt that God rejected my feelings of resentment, doubt, anxiety, and despair, and in the process also rejected me. So, I tried to deny or block out these feelings. This didn't work. It took a long time for me to recognize that when God accepts me, he accepts my "bad" feelings as well as the "good." Now I'm trying to accept my patterns of responding to situations and events. This permits me to deal with my feelings and drives within the context of my total living.

Similarly, I have had difficulty accepting my body. My religious indoctrination told me that the body is unimportant because it merely serves as a temporary housing for the spirit. The less one thought and said about the body, the better. But how can you ignore something that is so obvious and is with you all the time?

Some parts of my body have been harder to accept than others. My belly, for example, is an obvious reminder that I am not as self-disciplined as I ought to be. And I've always been overly self-conscious about my penis. In my teens, when I undressed for swimming or for football, I attempted to avoid exposing my pelvic area. Now I'm trying to accept my physical self, including these "hard-to-accept" parts.

I'm better able to accept my physical self when I remind myself that God created the whole package that is me, including my mind, spirit, and body. God created my belly and my penis. They're part of me; indeed, they're the only belly and penis that I have, and, it follows, I can appreciate them. I think everyone can profit from asking himself: "What part of me do I like best?" "What part of me do I have the most difficulty liking?" "Why do I feel as I do?"

There's another part of me that I have had difficulty accepting — my *needs*. Now I'm striving to accept not only my needs, but also my right to seek the satisfaction of my needs.4

My primary need is to survive, and this requires food, clothing, and shelter, among other things. Even my attempts to survive can be harmonious with my intention to live from the inside out — I work to earn money to acquire the things that will satisfy my basic needs. My inside-out approach also keeps me from confusing essentials with nonessentials: I don't con myself into regarding gourmet foods, flashy clothes, or a palatial home as essential to my existence.

When I have taken care of my survival needs, I become conscious of my psychological needs. I need warmth, loving care, stroking. I am acknowledging these needs more openly than before, and in the process I've become more human, making it easier for other persons to relate to me. For example, I recognize that I need to be appreciated. Although I make fewer conscious efforts to gain recognition than formerly, and although I don't feel so undone when praise isn't forthcoming, when someone *does* offer me a compliment, I accept it and appreciate it. I have scrapped that old neutralizing machine.

I also need to belong. I used to try to gain access to a group of significant persons by doing my "act," hoping that they would take notice and usher me into their midst. Now I feel free to tell a group that I'd like to join them and be a part of them. For example, I was invited to be a resource person at a seminar for ministers. It was a three-week course and I didn't arrive until the second week. In the past, the sweet taste of being a leader had been soured by my sense of being "other than." Arriving so late would have caused me to suffer considerable alienation. This time, I said to the group, "I'm here as a resource person, but I want to belong to the group and to participate in it, so I'll appreciate it if you'll help me to get acquainted and to share with you." Very quickly, I was accepted.

Beyond survival and belonging, I need to like myself and to express my uniqueness. To *accept* myself and to *appreciate* myself. It's been hard to lift myself out of my old patterns of self-rejection and self-punishment. Recently, when things seemed to be going bad and I was suffering depression, I said to myself, "Okay, Ben, what bad messages have you given yourself today?" The inherent humor of that remark evoked a chuckle. I recognized that I had let my low regard for myself poison my day. I made a new start and a brighter picture of myself and my situation emerged.

By expressing my feelings and drives, I become the person I'm destined to be. Another term for this is self-actualization. As a Christian, I see the self-actualizing process taking place in the dimension of spiritual awareness. As I listen to my needs, impulses, and drives, I seek to tune them so that they are in harmony with my total being. I am dependent upon the Holy Spirit for my understanding of what my true being is. I am becoming more and more convinced that my uniqueness does not derive from the peculiarities of my *needs* — indeed, my needs are surprisingly similar to your needs and everyone else's. My uniqueness arises out of the way that I go about *fulfilling these needs*. In other words, by my process of self-actualization.

I've struggled hard to become true to myself. Has all this effort been worthwhile? Yes! It has been worth the struggle if only for the sense of personal unity that I've gained. I used to feel at war with myself. (Paul has described this condition in Romans 7.) Self-acceptance has been a homecoming — I have come home to myself.

Another reward has been my deeper awareness of God's participation in all aspects of my life. I'm no longer reaching out to a God "out there" and inaccessible. Instead, God shares in my growth; he joins me in my struggles, rejoices in my successes, and reassures me of his love when I fail. I enjoy a unity with God.

I also enjoy a new unity with other persons. Formerly, it seemed that I was casting a net and pulling the other person to me. I had to climb into his skin. Together, we had to reshape our beliefs and behavior patterns until they were identical. Now I see that I can relate to other persons, yet permit them to be both different from me and separate. I am I; he is he; she is she. I resist the cloying togetherness which smothers individuality and ultimately causes estrangement.

Since I am less anxious than before, I am more willing to accept life's ebb and flow. There's an expression, "Don't push the river." I've been trying to enjoy the stream of life without feeling compelled to dam it, harness it, divert it. The stream of life flows in a wonderful and mysterious way, powerfully and dependably. Occasionally, I encounter rapids which excite me or quiet beauty which comforts me. These are the special times when the Spirit of God breaks into my life, bringing new illumination and inspiration.

In the next chapter, I want to write about these peak experiences and how they help me to gain a more valid view of who I am and who I am becoming. And in case you're concerned about my friend, the "retired successful business-man," and his question, "How can I discover more fully who I am on the inside?" I haven't forgotten them. I'll pick back up on our conversation in the next chapter, too.

looking through the slits in the fence
chapter 6

When I was a youngster, I didn't always have the price of admission to football games. But there were gaps in the weatherbeaten fence surrounding the old stadium, and by placing an eye at a slit, I could sneak a view of the game. It was an imperfect way to see a game, but better than not to see at all.

Sometimes a large spectator inside the fence moved in front of my slit, blocking my vision. Then I'd have to move to another slit. I had to move around anyhow if I was to see the crowd, the bands, and the various sections of the field itself. When a pass play was called, my slit of the moment might permit me to see the passer but not the intended receiver. I couldn't run to another slit fast enough to view the success or failure of the play. From the cheers or the groans of the crowd, I tried to guess the result. At best, this was frustrating.

This struggle to glimpse reality reminds me of some of my peak spiritual experiences. From what I see and hear, I know that something is stirring within the depths of my being that is fascinating and compelling, but I am unable to see the whole of it. I am standing behind the fence, looking through a slit. I catch glimpses but cannot see the whole picture.

The businessman whose "outside in" approach to life was related in the previous chapter had begun to get glimpses of spiritual reality through slits in the fence. His failure to find reality through postures and achievements had finally overwhelmed him.

"I might have gone under if it had not been for the spiritual discoveries that I began making in my life," he said.

His statement sparked my curiosity. Obviously, he had moved toward actualizing his spirit from within. Maybe he had already found an answer to his question, "How can I discover more fully who I am on the inside?"

"Tell me about your encounters with God," I said.

"As I reflect on my spiritual development, it seems to cover an awfully long time. The earliest serious search which I recall came during a laymen's conference. Several men in the church had encouraged me to participate. At the conference, I heard some talks which caused me to think seriously about God. I saw other men, not so different from myself, thinking and talking about the meaning of God in their lives. A lot happened to me during the retreat.

"As I drove home, I reflected on the experience. I began to fantasize. What would an experience with God feel like? How would I recognize it? How would it affect my life? Driving along, I had a serious experience of prayer. I wasn't disciplined, but I recall reaching out toward God.

"A few months later, I experienced the Spirit of God in a relational problem. I literally hated one of my business partners. I brought this strained relationship to God in prayer. After some changing on my part, I noted that my partner was also responding to me differently. God was confronting me not only in my solitary experiences, but also in my struggles in the business world. At the time, I didn't fully understand these experiences; certainly, I didn't know how to appropriate them.

"I began drawing closer to the church, and our minister asked me to teach a course in the new curriculum. For some reason that I still can't understand, I accepted responsibility for teaching a class in comparative Christology. The teaching material and my leadership role prompted an intellectual pursuit of Christianity which enlarged my vision. I saw that my inadequate concepts had often blocked a vital faith. My ideas had to be tempered with understanding before God could more fully reveal himself to me. For example:

"One evening, as I was studying, I felt the Spirit break into my life. I dashed into the living room and exclaimed to my wife, 'I really understand Harold DeWolfe's idea of perfect grace as a foundation for the incarnation!' I had grasped that truth rationally, and it gripped me emotionally. I lived in the glow of this experience the next few days.

"Up until this time, I had chosen to associate with persons like myself; in fact, I had adopted their life-style and most of their values. But when I began hanging around the church, I met a few Christians who embodied a different mentality. One of these was a young associate minister — a free, buoyant spirit, a really marvelous person. I was able to bounce my new ideas off him, and I heard him saying things that I never heard in the church before.

"Then, I encountered a lawyer in our congregation who was taking moral stands on race, politics, and government —

stands that were far from popular in our conservative community. I thought to myself, 'If I took those same stands, I would be fearful of losing the respect and companionship of my friends.' But this man either did not experience fear or did not let fear stop him. He seemed to live out of a source of inner strength, and I envied him.

"As I encountered the Spirit in these two persons, the associate minister and the lawyer, my hope of discovering a new and deeper dimension in my own life took bounding steps of confidence. And as my confidence grew, moments came when I seemed to glimpse my true self. I really wanted to open myself to God and to solicit his immediate presence, yet I increasingly became aware that the invasion of my spirit by the divine was not under my control.

"At the height of my search, I opened myself to God as fully as I knew how. I took an attitude of complete surrender. I don't mean that I forfeited responsibility for my life; rather, I opened myself to the divine Spirit, over which I had no control, and I responded to the Spirit out of the freedom God had given me. Still, no radical change in my pattern of living was apparent.

"But while I was in this attitude of openness, I attended another retreat. This weekend afforded me time to be alone and to reflect upon my growing concern for God. After this period of reflection, I felt a nearness to God. At times, my spirit seemed to be invaded by a divine presence. Let me tell you what it was like:

"I felt loved.

"I loved God.

"I felt a deep sense of forgiveness and acceptance.

"God seemed to say to me, 'I will guide your life; you are free to respond.'

"With this new sense of peace, I asked what I was to do. Immediately, an opportunity came for me to express my ministry through a witness on the city's Human Relations Commission. God spoke to me through persons in poverty that I didn't know existed. Because of the impact of these experiences, I began putting together a low-rent housing project. In this new approach to life, I seemed to be living from the inside out. Activated by the Spirit of God, I was doing what I really wanted to do, and I was doing it out of my own uniqueness. No longer was I seeking to gain the approval of others — not even God, for I knew I already had his approval.

"My new level of spiritual awareness became remarkably clear to me when I attended my first Lay Witness Mission in Chicago. As I met with the team, I felt reassured. I said to myself, 'Anything I might share with this group would get an OK response of love from them!' Accepting their acceptance afforded me a freedom I had never known before.

"After the mission, a friend and I were driving around Chicago in a borrowed car, seeing the sights and talking about the mission. As I contrasted the free style of life which I had glimpsed over against my former bondage to making money, I burst out with, 'I don't care about the money — let it all go!'

"In that moment, I felt free of the compulsion to make money, to seek position, to win the approval of my peers. I knew in a superrational way that I must pursue this new spirit dimension of life which was opening to me.

"That moment of freedom and spiritual awareness experienced in Chicago had an authentic ring. A few weeks later, however, my old mind-set came back into play. The value of the stocks which I owned tumbled, and to realize income, I was forced to sell several issues at half what I had paid for them. On Sunday, feeling anxious and depressed, I went to church. I wasn't attuned to the minister's talk, but as I sat in the Christian fellowship, I had a strong experience of God. I was guided to go home and reveal to my wife our financial decline. The thought of risking exposure frightened me. I had always been the strong businessman who could handle any situation. If I obeyed the Spirit, I might lose face.

"I was tempted to revert to 'outside-in' living; instead, I acted in the spirit. My wife gave me deep understanding. She reassured me that together we could make the decisions which would change our situation. Even today, when I recall that moment, I have a strong sense of the presence of God. As I opened my life to let my wife in, God came in with her.

"Since making money was no longer my primary goal in

life, I felt free to seek a vocation which would authentically express my being. It was important that I not seek to gain my identity through a new occupation, but rather seek a career which would best express my being. In my openness to a new vocation, I felt real freedom. I could say, 'I am a person who is free to pursue a vocational situation even if it is vague and uncertain. I am free to search for and find my identity as God reveals it to me.'

"The life of a self-actualizing person is one of uncertainty. In my previous 'outside-in' stance, it was always important for me to predict the future and then to project onto this picture of the future my aims and ambitions. This way, I forged a pattern of life that enslaved me. Now, instead of continuing this rigid, defensive style, with its limited possibilities, I resolved to be open to an awareness of the Spirit and the infinite variety of possibilities that openness offers, and to face up to the uncertainty that accompanies such openness.

"A door did open, and I made a vocational change. I stood in the office which I had vacated and said: 'God, I give all my life to you, my present and my future. I want to be a God-person who is sharing with you in your dream for man on this planet.' And God seemed to say, 'You are my much loved son; I am delighted with you.'"

I smiled at my friend. "Man, I can really appreciate what you've said. And I believe that you're in a much better position than I am to answer the question of what you're really like on the inside. I believe you already know."

What my friend had described was a series of peak experiences which provided clues to both his identity and destiny. My friend's experience is a model, for it describes graphically what thousands of other Christians have experienced in their search for wholeness. Something does happen when the divine Spirit encounters the human spirit. Through the slits in our lives' walls, we glimpse reality. We gain intimations of our identity and our destiny.

My own peak experiences have directed and sustained me in my quest for authentic personhood. (I have been influenced by A. H. Maslow's development of these ideas in *Toward a*

Psychology of Being.) Permit me to share some of my discoveries:

In peak moments, I feel "This is real!" My friend's Chicago experience was very real to him. This is the same reality that Jesus felt when he said, "I thank you, Father, that you always hear me."

In moments of intense spiritual awareness, I feel genuinely accepted. My friend felt that whatever he might share with the lay witness group would evoke an OK response from them. This was the acceptance which Jesus offered the woman who had been caught in adultery and was brought to him for judgment. She felt accepted when he said, "Neither do I condemn you; go and sin no more." The apostle Paul, in his experience of the Spirit, said, "The Spirit bears witness with our spirit that we are the children of God."

Moments of spiritual awareness give me a greater confidence in my own inspiration and intuition. I have begun valuing my own approval of myself above the approval of friends. With spiritual awareness has come courage to contradict commonly accepted standards of thinking and acting. Jesus had this overwhelming sense of confidence. "I do not speak from myself, but the Father which is in me. He is doing these works." Here is the courage to live from the inside out.

The presence of the Spirit enables me to detach myself from a situation so that I can view it more objectively. The Spirit led my friend to stand outside himself and view his relationship with his business associate. From this perspective, he saw that he had contributed to the hostile situation.

The Spirit enables me to rise above my negative feelings of the moment and to act on the basis of higher values. Jesus prayed, "Let this cup pass from me," but when it did not pass, he acted in obedience to the Spirit. The Spirit opens my eyes to the truth, and the truth makes me free. Brought to recognize my true life-values, I can resist contradictory pressures. Paul said, "Don't let the world around you squeeze you into its own mold, but let God remold your minds from within. . . ." (Romans 12:2, Phillips) Jesus resisted social rebuke and gave himself to the outcasts of his day. He let them know that they, too, were *somebody*.

When I have acted in harmony with the Spirit, I gain a sense of peace. Our businessman gained this sort of serenity. So did Paul: "The Spirit produces love, joy, peace. . . ." (Galatians 5:22)

To be awakened by the Spirit is, for me, like a resurrection. A new life. In his death and life, Jesus demonstrated that knowing God is the source of life.

The Spirit energizes me so that I become able to do things that, without the Spirit, I could not undertake or achieve. When I am in touch with the Spirit, I care about other persons so much that I am able to find creative ways to pursue ambitious projects to help others. My businessman-friend was motivated to establish a low-income housing project. Paul, a legalistic crusader, united with the people he formerly persecuted. Jesus did some of his greatest work following periods of peak awareness of God.

I can identify with Paul's description of looking through the slits in the fence: "Now we see through a glass dimly, but then face to face." My own peak moments provide a view of what it is like to live authentically; these same moments motivate me to seek to live out of this sense of identity and reality, even against tremendous odds.

My peak moments have led me to commit myself:

To be a real person.

To appreciate myself.

To remain open to the love of others.

To trust my own inspirations and creative urges.

To be objective when objectivity is indicated.

To be alive.

To share my Christian perspective with others in community.

These are the affirmations of a Spirit-actualizing person, and this is the kind of person I want to be. These intentions may seem bold, but they are not unreasonable. Many others have seen the same vision and have lived in the power of it.

Paul, in his first letter to Corinth, wrote about this same life-style: "As for a man, it is his own spirit within him that knows all about him; in the same way, only God's Spirit knows all about God. We have not received this world's spirit; we have received the Spirit sent by God that we may know all that God has given us." (I Corinthians 2:11-12, paraphrased.)

Paul says to me, "When the Spirit of God encounters your own spirit, then you will see clearly that God has given you a potential that is unlimited."

When my spirit meets God's Spirit, the slits in the fence widen and I gain an authentic glimpse of myself and my world. The view is vivid and real, and although it begins to fade with the passing of time, the memory of the moment lingers to draw me onward in life's adventures.

Peak experiences, then, provide us with clues to our identity; further, they sustain us as we live out of a sense of who we find ourselves to be. And the Spirit, during these peak encounters, leads us into communities which will participate with us in our efforts to actualize our unique personhood.

I look forward to seeing reality face to face, but for now I'm grateful for glimpses through the slits in the fence.

the courage to be me
chapter 7

On Christmas Eve, 1968, as three astronauts circled the moon, they gazed out of their craft to view an earth which seemed no larger than a 25-cent piece. Over television, they read aloud to fellow earthlings back home the first ten verses of Genesis: "In the beginning God created the heavens and the earth . . . the darkness and the light . . . the waters, the dry land, and the heavens . . . and God saw that it was good."

Mission commander Frank Borman had spent years preparing for this flight 240,000 miles into space. Yet, within seconds of the firing of the engines, the earth began falling away. Cities became barely discernible. Finally, the earth seemed no larger than a quarter. Borman and his two companions were seeing the earth as nobody had ever seen it before.

During peak experiences, I, too, have seen the world as it has never been seen before. This insightful moment may come as I contemplate a rose, a sunset, a baby's smile, or serenity in an old man's face. It may come in fellowship with a friend, or as I pray.

On such occasions, I glimpse reality. Sometimes in public, sometimes in private, I experience the shell splitting open, permitting me to see my true self — or the reality of life — or the love of God. And I recognize that although *similar* experiences happen to others, *this* experience is uniquely mine.

I can't describe fully the content of a peak experience, but I do know that God and the essence of life reach out and mesh with each other. In the presence of this phenomenon, I am electrified.

Although the glory of the moment ebbs,
   something of the richness remains with me;
I am left with a new understanding —
   a memory which conditions my life.
I have a new sense of direction,
   a new thrust.
This new burst of power erupting in me
   demands that I shove aside the self-imposed limitations
   which in the past have bound me.
But these revealing experiences
   also produce conflict:
Shall I act on the basis
   of the deep impulses which I have felt —
   the dazzling vision which I have seen?

Or shall I submit
   to my own "practical" estimates of myself
   and to reflections of myself
   that I read in other persons?
Shall I resume my "miserable creature" stance
   and live out of fear
   that I will be rejected by my peers?
Shall I slip back into the comfortable habits
   of adopting roles
   and playing it safe?
Or — dare I live
   from the inside out?

If I am to express my true being as *a unique, unrepeatable miracle of God*, I must develop the necessary know-how and skills. For me, this means four steps:

1. I identify clearly my feelings so that I may consciously act out of them.

2. I overcome the obstacles which I encounter in expressing my real self.

3. I identify sources from which I can draw strength for living a new style of life.

4. I take the risks that are involved.

Recently, I came to a place in my life which demanded a new beginning. The dreams of the last ten years had been fulfilled. I was at the end of an era. I was confronted with the question, "What will I do with my life? Where will I invest it?" These questions forced me to take a hard look at who I was on the inside.

While I was in this quandary, I happened to be in a distant city awaiting a flight home. I recalled a question that Bruce Larson had asked the participants at a conference: "If you knew that you could not fail, what one thing would you do with your life?"

If I knew that I could not fail, what would I do with my life? What would my life be like if I actualized it in obedience to God?

As these questions began challenging me, I heard an announcement that the flight to Atlanta was delayed two hours. Finding so much time on my hands, I decided to get in touch with my deepest self by giving flight to my imagination. I took out a notebook and began to write:

"What in life asks a response from me?

"Around me, in my fellow human beings, I see loneliness, hurt, and pain. I am personally and deeply aware of the emptiness and meaninglessness in which so many persons live. I have helped remove some of that hurt by enabling persons to get in touch with God and with each other. I would like to respond in a still greater way to loneliness, hurt, and meaninglessness."

Next, I wrote down some needs which are important to many people in our day. Then I began to list options through which I might help to fill these needs. I wrote:

"I can:

"Develop the Institute of Church Renewal as a national and international ecumenical organization on the frontier of the renewal of the church.

"Travel, speak to groups, train church leaders.

"Write a significant book out of my life experiences.

"Make creative programs available to churches and provide resources for implementing them.

"Develop a method for training leaders in renewal.

"Take a new interest in publishing books and tapes.

"Devote myself to underwriting resources for Christian endeavors.

"Develop a personal growth center.

"Develop models of house churches.

"Pursue a new and different career."

This list spanned the horizon of my interests and talents. I felt that I had the gifts or abilities to do any one of them. Each seemed an appropriate expression of myself, consistent with the understanding of myself that I have received in moments of spiritual awareness. I asked myself, "Who am I in relation to my life source, God? What activity would best express who I am at this time?" I considered several things that I know about myself:

I am deeply interested in persons, especially persons who are lonely and who hurt.

I am challenged by new ventures — things that I (and perhaps others) have never done before.

For me to embrace a project, it must promise to contribute to the realization of God's purpose for man. (That's what makes it meaningful for me.)

The task must be so challenging that there is a risk of failure.

I must ask myself, "Is this the one thing that God wants me to do?"

As I tested my list of options for personal ministry against these standards, I marked out several. When I ranked those that remained, two items emerged at the top of the list. One, to write a significant book. (This one. At least, it's significant to me.) And two, to create a method for training leaders in renewal.

As I mused over the idea of training, it became clear that I have no interest in building a building. I want to develop a mobile group of trainers who can equip today's church leadership for vital living and relevant ministry. As I tested that dream, it seemed right. I felt, "This is a task that I can give myself to with abandon."

In addition to this internal testing, I began to discuss the dream with friends. I listened for the Spirit of God in their responses. Significant persons said, "There's a need. I'm interested. I want to be a part of that dream." These responses confirmed that the Spirit was at work in me. My enthusiasm intensified.

With the idea growing, I began surveying my circumstances. "What opportunities are there to actualize this dream? What resources do I have?" As I answered these questions, I found a larger base for the project. I saw that it would complement all the other work of the Institute of Church Renewal. Now, a few months later, my dream is moving toward reality.

I have described here one method which I have used to identify my feelings as a unique creature of God. I first opened myself to dream the dream, then I brought my gifts to bear on that dream. The dream is consistent with who I am, what I want to do, and what I can give. When I approach life this way, I become aware of the Spirit acting in me, helping me to reconcile my interests and God's will.

If I am to be God's person, I must prepare myself for obstacles. Forces both inside and out menace my courage to express my uniqueness. Unless I recognize and deal with these obstacles, I will revert to living from the outside in.

For example, when I get in touch with my deepest being, I sometimes hear old "parent" voices. Let's say I have resolved that God loves me as I am. As I begin to act out of my sense of being loved, I hear a recording: "You had better be careful. Freedom is easily abused. If you get too chummy with God, you'll spoil things."

Recorded rules and regulations try to dampen the new-life impulses which stir in me. I act constructively when I turn down the volume of these fearful, circumscribing (but no longer appropriate) warnings; at the same time, I turn up the volume of the reality of God's love and acceptance of me. Now I can act with freshness, defying the long-implemented restrictions.

At other times, my vitality is beseiged from the outside. Family and friends may resist expressions of my being which seem to undermine their previously constructed images of me.

Let's consider a hypothetical situation. Suppose you have always been a submissive wife, letting your husband make the important decisions. If, for example, you have acquiesced to your husband's insistence upon spending Christmas with his relatives, he will experience a shock when you suggest remaining at home for the holidays — or visiting *your* relatives. The suggested change in your living pattern may shake him up, but it won't jar him nearly so much as will the implied change in your personality. Change will be an unwelcome visitor, and the two of you will have to renegotiate your relationship.

Even in Christian circles, friends may demand that you maintain a fixed life-style. I know a man who gave the impression that he never experienced anger. His friends extolled his patience and kindness. However, during a period of personal growth, he was amazed to discover that he harbored a great deal of hostility. Over the years, he had felt anger, but instead of identifying it and expressing it, he had pushed it into the basement of his mind. As years passed, the basement filled up. And when he began to unlock his anger and let it out, some of his friends were shocked. The fellow's new, authentic self contradicted his old image. One friend remarked to him, "You're not as good a Christian as you once were." Fortunately, other friends affirmed him and told him they experienced him as more real. Without this support, he might have retreated into his old pattern of suppressing his anger.

Old patterns vie with my new ways of acting. For years, I lived as a not-OK person and built my response to life on that basis. A few slashes at the weeds around me have not cleared the path to mature adulthood. But I am on my way, and to safeguard my journey, I intend to anticipate problems. To prepare myself, I have identified situations in which my undesirable patterns of thinking and acting assert themselves. Here are several examples:

When I am in the presence of significant persons, I feel an anxiousness akin to the insecurity that I felt as a youngster when I visited my city relatives.

When I am asked to speak to an important group, I often wonder if these persons will accept me.

When a significant person gets angry with me, I feel like a child who hasn't learned to handle feelings of rejection.

When I sense conflict with persons within a group, I feel overanxious and I overreact, trying to gain control of the group.

These are just a few of the situations that call forth automatic responses which are no longer acceptable to me. These responses prohibit spontaneity. The more of these "touchy" situations that I become aware of, the better fortified I can be.

As I have begun to live out of an OK stance, I have discovered a new range of feelings flowing into my consciousness. I need to (1) recognize and affirm the validity of these feelings, and (2) find appropriate ways of expressing them.

For example, I want to affirm my new feelings of self-worth and express them. In the past, I expressed negative feelings such as "I'm not what I ought to be." . . . "I'm not as good as so-and-so." . . . "Others can, but I cannot." Further, I sometimes find it difficult to express the new, self-confident me without an exaggeration which might suggest that I'm on an ego trip.

Another set of feelings which I am trying to deal with authentically has to do with my sexuality. When a person begins to be released through the Spirit, it isn't uncommon for him to become more aware of sexual feelings. Our society tends to give the child not-OK feelings about sex, and many of us grow up refusing to acknowledge our sexual feelings. But actualization through the Spirit releases a person from those not-OK inhibitions which are dehumanizing.

Some of us learn to be free in expressing our sexuality in marriage, but we feel anxious if we have sexual feelings toward a person not our spouse. To acknowledge sexual feelings does not mean we have to act on them; indeed, acknowledging the feelings and relating them to our sense of identity spares us from playing sexual games. I do not need to pursue an affair in order to prove my maleness. Indeed, the seductive use of sex often signals confusion and uncertainty regarding one's sexual identity. Free Christians can acknowledge and appreciate their sexuality without indulging in frustrating and painful games.

A friend of mine, having been taught that sexual feelings are evil, found it difficult to be around women whom he found attractive. When his sexual feelings asserted themselves, he was blocked from relating freely to the other person. I urged him to accept and appreciate his feelings. How much better to compliment a woman on her beauty, grooming, dress, or personality than to let negative and unresolved feelings undermine the relationship.

I believe that our sexuality is part of our uniqueness. I am learning to accept my sexual uniqueness, just as I accept the uniqueness of my voice. As a growing person, I want to accept my sexuality and to discover valid Christian ways for expressing it.

Let me generalize about feelings:

1. *Feelings are!* I do not elect whether or not to have feelings.

2. Feelings in themselves are neither good nor bad.

3. I am responsible for what I *do* with my feelings — not for *having* feelings.

4. I can identify my feelings and deal with them consciously and constructively.

As I have grown these last few years, I have less frequently experienced those "I have arrived" feelings which used to assert themselves whenever I clambered onto the next rung of the development ladder. Instead, I give myself a pat on the back, and then venture on. I do not fall in love with this new level, hang out a "Permanent Resident" sign, and begin developing a set of responses to go with my new position, thereby perpetuating it. I call the process of trying to encase one's feelings or actions in a protective shroud "cocooning."

This entrenching effect is a holdover from my earlier days. For example, during one period of my life, I repeatedly obtained release through a certain formula for prayer; I had one peak experience after another. The trouble was, I fell in love with the *method*. I laminated my prayer life between two sheets of plastic so that nothing could happen to it. In doing this, I unconsciously encased myself in plastic, too. I shut myself off from other opportunities for self-discovery and for open communication with other people.

Just as the caterpillar climbs to a new height on a bush and there shrouds itself in a protective covering, so we too attempt to encase the Spirit. When we have a peak moment, we take out a can of plastic spray and seek to preserve the moment exactly as it was. In the process, we also spray ourselves.

In the "prayer" cocoon which I constructed, I began to feel empty and lonely. I began to suspect that my seemingly safe environment wasn't so safe, after all. My cocoon began to sway. I played my old, soothing memory tapes in the effort to reassure myself that things were the same as always: "I've always been able to have an intimate encounter with the Spirit by engaging in my special prayer pattern," I said to myself, "so why should I doubt that the Spirit will continue to manifest himself to me in this way?"

Life cannot be frozen; when I freeze any aspect of my being, I die a little. And the Spirit, especially, refuses to be immobilized. So my frozen prayer life prevented me from receiving new manifestations of the Spirit.

My fear and frustration made me aware that I was out of touch with the source of my being. But to get in touch again was not enough. I also had to learn how *to act out of* the new feelings.

When I test my new patterns of behavior, my old patterns clamor to take over. Here I am, trying to be a free person, yet I get these negative signals from within and outside. How shall I deal with these signals? Shall I build myself a cocoon?

Fortunately, there are supports which encourage me to be my real self. I find strength, for example, in persons who model a spontaneous, authentic life-style. Observing them gives me hope that I, too, can be really free.

One of the freest spirits I know is William S. Taegel. Bill and I have worked together, struggled together, wept together, rejoiced together. In recent years, Bill has made radical changes in his life-style. He has emerged a free, uninhibited, playful person — quite a contrast from the person that I knew a decade ago. Then he was locked in a rigid, hard-disciplined code of behavior. Bill has let his "child" come out to play. When I am with Bill, I appreciate life more — indeed, I *am* more alive. And I want to grow to the point where I will celebrate my personhood all of the time, just as I do when I'm with Bill.

Let me tell you about another reassuring personality, Jim Laney. As you might imagine, an innovative ministry draws barbs. I have felt rejected by the "establishment" so often that I probably expect rejection in advance and prematurely marshal a defense. When Jim Laney became dean of the Candler School of Theology of Emory University, I felt it expedient to get acquainted with him, outline my own ties with Emory, and describe my ministry — before some critic did.

At lunch, I began telling Jim about the Institute. I'm sure there was apology in my voice. But right off, I sensed that

Jim was affirming me. I didn't need to defend myself. And the more we talked, the more comfortable I became. Never before had I encountered a person who so quickly communicated total acceptance.

Later, as I reflected on our meeting, I came upon the source of Jim's gift of accepting others: This man had come to terms with *himself*. He had accepted himself so completely that he didn't mind making himself vulnerable. Consequently, he didn't need to place conditions on our new relationship. He didn't need to say, "Well, I want us to have a good relationship, but of course we'll want to lay down some ground rules."

By his example, Jim Laney has encouraged me to enable other persons to be themselves.

Another supportive element for me I've already described at some length in this book — peak experiences.

As my spirit encounters the Spirit of God, I stand outside myself and view my situation free of blinding and binding limitations. Sometimes I seem to be standing on a ridge looking back upon a valley where rests my past and then looking across to a mountain representing my path into the future. Each peak experience expands and reinforces my vision of myself as a person who worships and obeys God. While the experiences vary in their content, duration, and intensity, I invariably receive:

— A new sense of who I am.
— Reassurance of the reality of God.
— A new vision of life.
— A surer sense of my direction.

Although I choose to remain open to these peak experiences, I remind myself to avoid seeking the experiences for themselves. They are always a gift, so attempting to work for them is self-defeating.

Still another supporting element in my life is the caring community. Such a place is the safest environment for me to try out my new concepts and new patterns of behavior. Such a community needn't be large; it can be just one other person and myself. But there is no limit (although very large numbers tend to preclude intimacy), and a caring community may comprise a church school class or a prayer group. What counts isn't the *quantity* of persons, but the *quality* of the relationships. Perhaps you are part of a community in which you're able to reveal your deepest hopes and fears. The community hears your feelings as well as the intrinsic content of your words. You can make yourself vulnerable without fear you'll be devastated.

Let me cite an example. In a community of which I am a part, one member had a dream of a retreat center. It was an ambitious project, and he feared that the community might reject it as ridiculous — either that, or politely let it die a slow death. But when he mentioned his aspiration to the community, he found immediate support. "How do you see this retreat center being developed?" one member asked. "How can we help?" inquired another. Instead of experiencing rejection, he found understanding and encouragement.

The caring community affords enough security for me to test new patterns of behavior. For example, I can identify and express feelings of anger. Also, I can accept compliments and celebrate achievements without embarrassment.

Finally, I find support in the good news — the OK Gospel. The good news embraces the various supportive influences which I have already described, plus others.

The good news reminds me that God created man to *live*, not simply to be religious. Man is to live in obedient response to God's purpose for him; within this context, he is also to live aggressively and courageously out of his own sense of identity and self-worth. Life is to be relational rather than legalistic — thus the importance of a community in which freedom can be exercised without fear of being wiped out.

The good news tells me that I am an agent for change and a creator of history. Tied with this is my freedom to fail — I would never be able to risk if I were not afforded the opportunity to fail without being condemned.

Freedom to fail! The lack of it was for so many years my undoing. For me to understand and accept the fact that I am permitted — even expected — to fail is indeed *good news*. This good news has enabled me to turn my life around and head it in a new, more fulfilling direction.

whose voice do I listen to?
chapter 8

The inspiration which I gain from peak spiritual experiences invariably comes under attack from negative forces both within and outside, so I have learned to be on guard. No sooner has God encouraged me to live a more daring life than my old patterns of thinking and behaving assert themselves. However, the tug-of-war which ensues isn't altogether unproductive; by testing both sides of issues, I refine my concept of who I really am.

One of Jesus' peak experiences was his baptism. Imagine yourself among the throngs alongside the river. You hear John say, "I don't feel that I should baptize you; rather, I need you to baptize me."

The stranger says, "Go ahead, because it is the right thing to do."

The two go into the water. As they emerge, you notice a glow on the face of Jesus. Then you hear God speak: "You are my beloved Son in whom I am well pleased."

This peak experience of Jesus was not earned; it was a gift from God, spontaneous and free. It is precisely this sort of experience that affirms our identity. If, in that moment, you had asked Jesus who he was, he would have answered, "I am God's son. God has accepted me, and he has destined me for a life of fulfillment."

Imagine what such an unequivocal sense of identity and purpose can mean to you. You know who you are. You glimpse the meaning of your life. You know your direction.

After this peak experience, the Spirit took Jesus into the wilderness for a tempering of his new gift of identity. Jesus was tempted to repudiate his understanding of himself.

The adversary said, for example, "If you are the Son of God, turn these stones into bread." But Jesus knew that his physical needs were not his ultimate concern, so he refused to gratify himself through the miraculous process. Instead, he responded, "Man is not meant to live by bread alone."

The next human characteristic to come under scrutiny was the need for esteem. Jesus was urged to leap from the pinnacle of the temple — a show of power sure to charm the people. But Jesus refused. To seek gratification of his need for esteem in so flamboyant a manner would have been an insult to his identity and vocation.

Again and again, Jesus lived true to God's purpose for him, as affirmed in the baptism experience. He refused to seek his identity from outside sources through performance. Jesus just kept on acting as the Son of God. He continued to live from the inside out.

The post-peak-experience battle which Jesus won, many of us lose. I know that following peak experiences I often let renegade patterns of behavior take over. The contradiction between the voices-from-the-past and the me-of-the-present causes static in my life. Sometimes the turmoil causes an overload of not-OK feelings, immobilizing me. Then I know that I have a long way to go in my quest for maturity.

If I am to follow Jesus' model, I must tune down the negative voices and tune up the positive. This is precisely what Dr. Harris recommends in his *I'm OK — You're OK*.[5]

Harris says there are three ego states: (1) the parent, (2) the child, and (3) the adult. In any period of his life, a person may act out of any of these states.

When I function out of my *parent* ego state, I am dogmatic, judgmental, authoritarian. My parent issues rule. My parent speaks of "good" and "bad," "right" and "wrong," "truth" and "error."

When my *child* ego state takes over, I act out of my feelings, for my child is my feeling self. In my child are stored feelings of anxiety, fear, hostility — and feelings of confidence and joy. My repertoire of feelings was put together during my earliest experiences of trying to fulfill my needs, and these patterns have been reinforced through repetition.

Although my *adult* ego state began forming long before I became an adult, it represents a higher, more sophisticated stance. In my adult state, I am able to question both the rules and directives of my parent nature and the feelings of my child side and to update them with newer, more accurate information. My parent and child have their values, but it is in my adult state that I exercise my personal freedom to determine who I am and how I will express my sense of personhood.

To visualize this concept, picture the brain of a child as a stereophonic tape recorder. There are two tracks on the tape, and, by using two microphones, two recordings can be imprinted simultaneously.

One microphone is held by the child's parents and parent-surrogates. Their messages to the child are recorded in high fidelity; importantly, they are not edited — that is, they are not evaluated and altered by the child. The parent track cannot be erased; it can only be turned down.

The second microphone is wired to the child's feelings. As the child attempts to fulfill his needs, he experiences feelings about himself and his world, and these feelings are recorded "raw," just as the parent impulses are. This feeling track cannot be erased, either; it can only be turned down.

Now, when the child (who may have long since become an adult) runs into a situation similar to a situation from his past, his tape player automatically begins playing back the parent and child channels. The trick is for the child (or the grown person he has become) to shift into the adult ego state and to test these old messages in terms of his present understanding of himself and his world. In other words, to shift from "automatic" controls to "manual" controls.

For most of my life, I let my parent and child tapes dictate my thinking and behavior. I wasn't discerning enough or strong enough to intervene. It was easier for me to function as I always had. But gradually I began challenging these voices from my past; ever so timidly at first, I began turning down the volume of my parent and child recordings and turning up the volume of my adult position. My peak experiences encouraged me and supported me as I began to explore the possibilities for self-actualization in lieu of puppetlike responses to persons around me.

Perhaps you have encountered my problem. Maybe the Spirit has given you a new vision of who you are and can become. But almost immediately, you are beset by voices from the past which tell you that you are something less than the Spirit has suggested. You want to say "yes" to the Spirit and live out of a sense of OK-ness, but you fear that you will succumb to your old ways. Let me spare you some of the pain and effort I have experienced in my own struggle to express my true self in contradiction of alien voices.

Understand, I do not offer this counsel out of a stance of "having arrived," but rather as one who is on the journey.

■ I tune in on my feelings, identifying them and trying to determine how I came to feel as I do.

■ Once I have identified a feeling and understand the influence which triggers it (for example, when someone poses as an authority, I become resentful because my father was authoritarian and this caused me pain), I decide what I am going to do about this feeling. Is it a feeling that I am comfortable with, one that complements my new sense of my selfhood — or is it negative and destructive? If it's an OK feeling, then I want to embrace it; if it's a not-OK feeling, then I choose not to act on it. This approach to my feelings is adult.

■ I listen to my parent tapes and identify the admonitions and restrictions which they contain. Moreover, I recall the source and context.

■ I decide what I am going to do about these voices which speak to me of "good" and "bad," "can" and "can't." Does this admonition or limitation fit my situation today and serve a good purpose, or is it an empty edict which no longer applies? If it's an OK rule, then I want to embrace it; if it's a not-OK command, I want to ditch it and make a new directive permitting myself to live spontaneously.

■ I integrate my new understandings of my feelings and my parent impulses and begin living out of my new, adult stance.

I have had difficulty getting in touch with my feelings and deciding what to do about them. Most of the time, I didn't understand what was going on inside me — I was afraid to probe and find out. So, when negative feelings arose, I disowned them and pushed them down inside me; as a result, they blocked my relationships and caused pain for me and for other persons.

Harris tells me that my negative feelings are in my not-OK child. When, as a child, I attempted to obtain fulfillment of my needs, I often ran into obstacles or ridicule. The resentment, hurt, or fear which I experienced was picked up on my child tape without evaluation or editing. It helps for me to understand that when I experience feelings today, I can usually trace the roots of these automatic responses to specific segments of my development.

I've learned to ask myself four questions:

1. What am I feeling?
2. When did I feel this way before?
3. Is today's situation the same as that earlier situation?
4. In my present situation, do I want to embrace the feeling or turn down its volume and begin a new evaluation?

Let me illustrate. One evening, I came home to find my wife angry with me because I hadn't picked up my clothes that morning. My response was to feel defensive and a bit frightened.

In earlier days, I would have been undone by these negative feelings. As a child, I would have been motivated to run off and hide, or to offer excuses, or to whimper or cry. But this time, I paused and tried to sort out my feelings and ascertain why I had them. Meanwhile, I affirmed that I had heard my wife by saying to her, "I want to respond, but I don't know how I should respond just now. Will you give me a minute to get in touch with what I'm feeling before I express myself?"

I asked myself, "When have I felt like this before?" I felt like this whenever my mother corrected me. My mother was good, and her influence in my life was so powerful that in her presence I felt little, weak — and condemned. My mother was a significant woman in my life, and so was my wife. It follows that I was responding to my wife as I responded to my mother when she rebuked me.

But then I applied the "reality" test. "Is this present situation the same as the past situation?" And the answer was, "No, it isn't." I am not dependent upon my wife as I was my mother. My wife and I are interdependent. My wife cannot paddle me or banish me to my room; therefore, I don't need to act defensively. I can accept myself as an OK person — although a bit untidy at times.

"You know, I really ought to pick up after myself, and I want to learn to do this," I said.

Not only did my shifting to an adult, or mature, stance help me to overcome the specific problem — it also enabled me to see that I was probably bringing a mother image to my wife in many other situations. I resolved not to confuse these two roles.

In this instance, I successfully identified my feelings; traced their roots; tested their validity; decided that they did not apply; updated my "child" with this new, "adult" information, and acted out of this more authentic understanding.

But this is just one incident and I encounter hundreds of such experiences every week or so. The prospect is not so forbidding if I permit myself to relish any bit of progress that I make — such as my growth from resolving this clothes-picking-up confrontation.

I am trying to deal with my parent tapes in a more adult, more responsible way. You will recall that the "absolute-truth" admonitions of my parents and my parent-figures were recorded without editing. Recall also, please, that these recordings were made while I was in a life-stance of "You're OK but I'm not okay."

When my parent tapes play, I hear things like:

"Never discuss family affairs with outsiders."

"A job that's worth doing is worth doing well."

"Don't start something that you can't complete."

My parent tapes tell me what to do, what not to do; where to go, where not to go. At the time the messages were recorded, I didn't challenge their validity — thus, I have to interpret and evaluate them now.

As I listen to my parent assertions of "must," "should," "always," and "never," I have to decide which of the recordings remain authentic under the present circumstances. Some of the admonitions are still valid and should be affirmed, while others are grossly inappropriate and should be deemphasized.

As I deal with my parent tapes, I follow essentially the same procedure that I followed in relating to my child tapes.

1. I identify the parent message and the voice.

2. I ask whether today's situation is the same as the past situation.

3. I ask whether the parent message is constructive in view of my new understanding of myself and who I'm trying to become.

4. I resolve either to turn down the volume on this parent message or to let it play.

One tricky aspect of evaluating "shall" and "shall not" imperatives is ascertaining whether they arise out of the parent life-stance or adult life-stance. A directive which arises out of a mature, conscious evaluative process (adult) certainly requires less scrutiny than a directive which was recorded "raw" while I was in my not-OK life-position (parent). But any decision is subject to review and updating. After evaluation, the directive can be fully or conditionally accepted, or fully or conditionally rejected. This is not to say that the directive will be erased — it won't. But the point is, when the admonition does play, I will be able to recognize it for what it is and pay only so much attention to it as it deserves.

Let me give you an example of one of my parent-updating experiences.

At Emory University, I completed the residence work for a Ph.D. degree — I passed two language exams, did the course work, and passed five, five-hour preliminary exams. All that remained between me and the degree was the writing of a dissertation.

For six years, I worked on my dissertation, but never with total concentration. There were too many distracting influences. Also, my unconscious may have been resisting the effort. But during these six years, I never permitted myself to think of abandoning my pursuit of the doctor's degree.

The seventh year, I did nothing to complete my dissertation. Then, at the beginning of my eighth year — the last year in which I could complete my degree requirements — I acknowledged that for the last several years I had not wanted to go on with this degree project.

Why hadn't I been honest with myself? Because I heard parent tapes lecturing me: "Don't start something that you can't complete" and "A job that's worth doing is worth doing well."

But when I examined these admonitions, I saw that they were not authentic expressions of my identity, nor did they promise to fulfill my sense of destiny. Earlier, the need for a degree may have been very real, but not now. In the interim, I had become immersed in lay witness activities and other church-renewal work. I didn't need a Ph.D. to prove my worth, nor could I spare the time to complete my dissertation. I turned down the volume on my parent tape and abandoned my plan to acquire a Ph.D.

The updating of my parent tape was essential. If I had continued to pursue the degree (whether or not I was awarded it) without updating the parent tape, I would have suffered self-estrangement.

An evaluation of child and parent tapes does not invariably lead to their rejection. For example, there are feelings associated with childhood which remain valid expressions of who I am and who I want to become. Examples: I want to cultivate my sense of wonder and I want to embrace my inclinations to laugh or to cry. I want to be fully human.

Similarly, I will not abandon good principles just because they first came into my consciousness while I was a dependent child. It's still valid to love the church, respect my elders, and look both ways before crossing the street.

But the point is, I now bring my adult understanding of myself to bear on the feelings and commandments which I acquired in not-OK moments. I slip under the wheel and command the driver's seat. I cannot let inappropriate feelings and rules and regulations commandeer my life and carry me along as a captive passenger.

I see Jesus being truly adult, the foremost expert on living out of one's sense of identity. He wasn't hooked on defensive patterns of thinking or behaving. He was always the person that God intended him to be.

I believe that just as I am a unique and miraculous creature of God, so also do I have a unique and wonderful destiny. But I am not living up to my identity or my destiny when I either costume myself in outdated trappings or contemptuously cast aside authentic apparel just because it isn't new.

I want to throw myself out onto the horizons of each day. Realistically, however, I know that I have a trunk full of unsorted relics on my back. I must go through this clutter and get rid of the junk, else the burden of it will sap my strength and jeopardize my journey.

The voice of the Spirit — my adult voice — tells me to get on with my personal growth.

free-style living
chapter 9

As the worship service of our church began, the leader asked each of us to stand rigidly with our arms wrapped around our chest and shoulders, our chin frozen against our chest, and our eyes clamped shut. When we had stood in this awkward position for a couple of minutes, the leader asked,

"How does this feel to you? Get in touch with your body. Listen to what your body is telling you about living and experiencing this frozen position."

My arms and shoulders ached. My chest was numb. The back of my neck felt strained beyond hope of recovery. I felt a tightness in my head. I also felt isolated from every other person in the room. I felt anxious over my simulated blindness and having to maintain this cramping posture.

The leader asked us to move quietly around the room, making contact with other persons, blindly bumping and touching. Some people related to one another with the brush of an elbow or a jostling of hips. I was too uncomfortable to throw myself into such an encounter.

Finally, the leader said, "I am now going to take steps to release you from this cramped style in which you find yourself. I will release one person among you by saying to him, 'God loves you and accepts you. In the name of Christ, be released and free.' This person will open his eyes, relax his arms, and straighten his chin. Then he will perform the same ministry to another person, setting him free, and on and on until all of you are free."

My anxiety heightened. *What if I'm the last person to be released?* Soon, however, a brother touched me on the shoulder and said, "God loves you and accepts you. In the name of Christ, be released and free." I opened my eyes. My rescuer unfolded my arms, lifted my head, and invited me to celebrate symbolically the freedom that Christ affords his followers. I celebrated!

As our small congregation discussed insights from playing this simulation game, most of us said the exercise had been helpful. We had experienced two contrasting life-styles — one closed, the other open; one frozen, the other free. The closed-and-frozen style expresses the not-OK person, struggling under the demands of the Not-OK Gospel. The open and free life-style characterizes the OK person, made whole by the Gospel of OK. The game held meaning for me because I have lived the closed style and am only now discovering how to live the open style. Let me describe how the two styles oppose each other:

OPEN STYLE	CLOSED STYLE
I live in the here and now, expecting to meet God in current encounters.	I tend to blur the present with memories of the past or expectations of the future.
I have realistic expectations of myself; I genuinely accept my whole self, including my feelings and fantasies.	I expect more of myself than I can produce; when I do approach my expectation, I raise the goal, thereby guaranteeing failure.
I recognize and accept alternation — privacy-togetherness, work-rest, seriousness-play, peak moments-bland moments, giving-receiving, pain-pleasure — as part of the human situation, tending to enrich life.	I am afraid of change. Each shift in mood or involvement raises the question of whether or not I am doing the will of God. I feel best about myself when I am in a serious mood (for example, when I'm dealing with a weighty problem). When I feel playful, I fear that God is frowning upon me.
I welcome new experiences, new relationships, new feelings, and new responses to life.	I shut out new experiences because they threaten my sense of security. I seek a safe shelter.
I can function in different roles at different times, according to the need. I can be father, son, husband, minister, manager, subordinate. I am flexible.	I see myself having a single, rigidly defined role. I cling to this role however inappropriate it may be.
I meet other persons as my equals and place few restrictions on our relationship.	I approach other persons as either their superior or inferior. I draw lines to limit the relationship.

OPEN STYLE	CLOSED STYLE
I project an honest communication of myself to others. My nonverbal signals complement my words.	I endeavor to project an ideal image. My words contradict my real feelings.
I am true to my self-identity, hoping that I'll be accepted just as I am.	I seek to achieve acceptance through performance.
I approach life with trust in God, in life's circumstances, in myself, and in other persons.	I meet life with fear; I am suspicious of God and life itself; I distrust my own motives and those of others.
I see unlimited possibilities for self-discovery, spiritual exploration, creativity, and fulfillment.	I am constrained by past disappointments and hurts.

As we become whole, we search for a life-style that will be commensurate with our new sense of being. A not-OK person may compulsively cling to his old ways because the closed style seems to provide him with security. But a free person, acting out of his inner being and celebrating life, will throw off such restrictions. He will move toward an open posture which permits him flexibility in expressing his uniqueness.

In this chapter and the next, I would like to explore with you the nature of open-style living.

Living in the Here and Now

The whole person lives in the here and now with realistic expectations of God, himself, and other persons. The not-OK person tends to live either in the past (with unpleasant memories) or in the future (in fantasy).

I was discussing this point with a friend. She said, "I often find myself enjoying an experience more in retrospect than while it's happening." It seems to me that my friend feels safer when the present has been resolved (it then becomes the past). She does not enjoy coming to grips with the present or looking toward the future. On the other hand, I find it more comfortable to anticipate my future than to reflect upon my past or to savor the present. In the midst of celebration, I find myself anticipating the next achievement.

There was a time when I frequently was driven into the future by not-OK feelings. The future orientation of the Not-OK Gospel appealed to my not-OK-ness. At the time of my conversion, I received the gospel as condemnation: I was a sinner who had failed God, and I was lost. I appreciated Christ's loving me enough to die for me, but it seemed strange that so great a man would give up his life for a wretch like me. I felt guilty.

In my position of a not-OK Christian, I presumed that I would have to work myself out of purgatory-on-earth through abject selflessness, rigorous piety, and good works. To this end, many well-meaning people handed me lists of do's and don'ts. Not only did they fail to identify the lists as being their own creations; they also implied that the rules had universal application. The code that was recommended to me was reinforced in the preaching that I heard and in the Christian discussions which I attended.

I didn't measure up, but I couldn't afford to acknowledge my failure or question the validity of the goals — when I did, I suffered guilt. I labored to keep my "Christian" image intact, inside and out.

I became aware of a strange psychological mechanism at work. Whenever I neared a goal, I raised the specifications. At the time, I couldn't fathom what was happening, but now I know that my picture of a devout Christian required him to crawl up a never-ending mountain over jagged rocks in intolerable heat and cold, gasping for breath and bleeding profusely, and beating on his chest and pleading for forgiveness all the while. I punished myself. Moreover, filled as I was by negative feelings that were both self-generated and foisted upon me, I imposed rigorous standards upon others in my community. What we had going was a Mutual Rejection Society.

The only route to recovery which I could see was for me to confess to God what a terrible sinner I was and to pray myself out of my condemned condition. Obviously, I wasn't giving God much to work with, and I oftentimes felt even more rejected following my devotions and prayers. I projected my negative feelings about myself into God and into other persons: "They don't accept me."

I call this cycle the "Failure Syndrome." I have not-OK feelings; I hear the gospel as bad news; I view mankind as hopeless. I desire to reach spiritual perfection; I want to understand all the tricky implications of the Bible; I want to straighten out the sinners around me.

But how can anyone reach perfection when he undermines the base of his unique personhood; stands with one foot clamped on the other; sees God pressing down on the top of his head with the palm of his huge hand, and imagines a host of friends and acquaintances pulling upon him for spiritual support?

Haunted by a painful past and burdened with a pleasureless present, I grativated toward a future time and place of serenity, fulfillment, and release. If I could just hold on and *exist* through this life, I could *live* in the next. *What a prostitution of the Christian message of love, acceptance, and life!*

Once I came around to the concept of living here and now, I had to junk my unreal expectations — expectations like:

Because I am a Christian, I have all the answers.

I know what God wants of my life, specifically and eternally.

There will be no mysteries that God will not explain to me.

If I'm a good enough Christian, God will spare me from suffering, economic reversals, and personal anxiety.

Since I know what is right and what is wrong, I have only to follow the rules and I'll never be guilty of sin.

If I don't live a good and proper life, God will inflict a more severe punishment upon me because I "knew better."

A Christian community is a group of persons who have individually gotten right with God.

If I read the Bible and pray, I won't have any doubts about

God and his ways — which is good news, since to doubt is to sin.

Through self-denial, I will rise above sexual feelings.

These expectations are false (and some of the goals to which they look are of dubious value). They are rooted in aspirations for perfection, and perfection is an unrealistic — and cruel — standard. The goal is set too high, the performance falls short, and guilt and frustration ensue.

Here, on the other hand, are some realistic expectations:

I am a creature of God and I receive his continuing love as a gift even when I fail to live up to standards set either by myself or other persons.

I will make mistakes; I will even fail at some major projects — but God has provided me with judgment and will, so I always have another crack at doing better.

As I seek to actualize my unique personhood, I have the support of God and of other persons.

Although I will have enduring relationships, none will remain static (something else for me to be thankful for).

By living an open life in which I embrace both pleasure and pain, I will discover new heights of intimacy, creativity, spontaneity, wisdom, productivity, and enriched personhood.

Although an open life-style is predicated on venturing and risking pain and failure, it is at the same time the life-style which affords the most excitement and fulfillment.

These are my expectations as I attempt to live in the here and now.

Living in the Cycles of My Life

A second major characteristic of the open style of living is acceptance of alternation and cycling. The careful observer sees in the natural world and in civilization many pairs or sets of contrasting conditions which appear, wane, disappear, and reappear. The open life-style recognizes the values of alternation and cycling, whereas the closed style tends to regard many of life's pendulum-swings and checks and balances as negative or excessive. Here are some seemingly opposing circumstances which actually blend to give life zest and completeness.

Privacy-togetherness. I need times of quiet reflection in which to "get in touch with myself." But I also need to be intimate with and share with other persons. Many of us tend to pursue the one and neglect the other. I tend to be a "people" person, neglecting my need for solitude, while others that I know tend to be loners. Our needs are individualistic; still, we must experience both privacy and togetherness if we are to be healthy and productive persons. I don't think I would be at my best as a hermit, on the one extreme, or as a member of a full-sharing commune, on the other.

Work-rest. The biblical record declares, "In six days God made the heavens and the earth and on the seventh day he rested." God emphasized productive activity, but he also consecrated one day as a memorial to rest. The Judeo-Christian tradition places value on both work and rest, but our not-OK-ness sometimes causes us to tie our worth to practical achievement, relegating leisure to a subordinate and even "sinful" role.

Are the work and leisure aspects of my own life in balance? I must confess that if I review my average week, I will look back more fondly on some important task than some recreational activity or restful moment. I tend to feel uncomfortable out of harness, and I probably keep myself too heavily engaged in professional enterprises and serious attempts at self-improvement. I herewith resolve to approach my leisure opportunities more creatively.

Serious engagement-playful abandon. Most of my life, I was a sober, serious, and (I'm afraid) somber person. In my early Christian life, I thought that my every waking moment ought to be spent winning souls for Christ, and I engaged in this pursuit with grim determination. How could I justify frivolity and games when there were millions of lost souls — souls for whom I was personally accountable?

I no longer feel that God means for me to be deadly serious all the time. He means for me to express the moods which come and go in open-style living. I no longer feel that God holds me responsible for either the salvation or the welfare of all other men. Persons *are* important — if I didn't think they were, I would spend my time differently. But my new perspective is that I can be responsible *to* another person, but not responsible *for* him. I'm his brother, not his keeper.

During my early Christian life, I often wore a detached or pained look as part of my Christian insignia. Now I know that reserve and stiffness are contrary to my true nature, and I know that God doesn't want me to go around pretending.

The OK person acknowledges the importance of both serious engagement and playful abandon, and he expresses each appropriately in season. Moreover, because he is OK, he encourages other persons to be true to their moods.

Peak experiences-valley experiences. Another myth which, I am delighted to say, exploded in my face was my early misconception that the Christian was supposed to live on the mountaintop all or most of the time. Such an expectation is not realistic; moreover, it isn't biblical. All of the spiritual giants experienced famine as well as feast; for all their shining moments, there were days when life lacked luster and when they questioned whether life made sense and even whether God had wandered off somewhere and forgotten all about them.

Since I am a creature of God and am equipped with a full range of emotions, I expect to feel estrangement as well as closeness, doubt as well as certainty, low pot as well as full pot. To feel that God is upset with me when I am in a questioning mood is to deny that I am to experience and express the full range of human feelings. I certainly prefer my peak moments to the times when I bottom out, but I remind myself that I should celebrate my lows as well as my highs. I don't believe God places a star on my calendar every time I have a peak experience and a black mark for a valley visit.

Giving-receiving. "It is more blessed to give than to receive." It's no wonder that I became immersed in that declaration early in my Christian life, for I heard it almost every Sunday. I was deeply impressed with the benefits which would accrue to the cheerful giver. (Many evangelists who visited our town suggested practical returns as well as spiritual rewards.)

I recall feeling deep sympathy for a widow who was struggling alone to rear a daughter. Being a responsive young Christian who happened to be blessed with a small bank account, I went to the bank and withdrew $10 and gave it to this woman. Seriously, this was a good experience for me. I didn't tell anyone of this act, which is something in my favor. However, I'm not sure I should have relished my sacrifice for such a long, long time afterward.

I really like to give to other people. When someone resists letting me buy his lunch, I have a standard rejoinder: "How can there be cheerful *givers* if there are no cheerful *getters*?"

Did not Jesus say, "For even the Son of man came not to be ministered unto but to minister and to give his life a ransom for many"? In addition to Jesus' supreme giving, I was deeply impressed by the life of sacrificial living modeled by Jean Valjean in Victor Hugo's great novel *Les Miserables.*

I've been a much better giver than receiver, and this worries me. I can rationalize that giving runs truer to my nature. But I must also confess a suspicion that I shun receiving because it makes me feel weak and vulnerable, while giving makes me feel strong and contributing. When I'm on the receiving end of the transaction, I cannot always be sure about the motives of the giver, or the indebtedness which I will feel, or the demands which my benefactor may place upon me in return. In other words, I'm unwilling to risk — and that's contrary to an open life-style.

Why can't I accept gifts generously just as I give generously? Why can't I let another person enjoy the same good feelings that I experienced when I gave $10 to that widow?

I know some persons who need to work at the other side of the equation. I once had a friend who wasn't just *accepting* — he was *expecting.* He received and received, but he never gave. Our relationship withered. The open life-style is dedicated to neither giving nor receiving exclusively; it seeks *sharing*.

Alternation is the spice of life. It gives life balance and reason. How can I fully relish a moment of ecstasy if I have never known what it is to feel worthless? How can I appreciate the soothing, healing power of rest if I have never worked until I was dog tired?

Alternation and cycling are integral parts of life. I embrace them as part of God's plan, whether convenient or inconvenient, pleasurable or painful.

In the next chapter, we will continue to examine the building blocks which make for a free life-style.

more on the free life-style
chapter 10

For seven years, a childhood friend of mine was a prisoner of the North Vietnamese. Seven years! Think about it. In that length of time a child can move from birth into the second grade. Or a new high school graduate can earn a doctorate. A couple can marry, build a home, start a family. In seven years, a person can do an awful lot of living!

By most standards, my friend did a lot of *existing*. He was physically cramped and deprived. Worse, he was psychologically and emotionally constrained. His days and nights were endless stretches of drab sameness. And when there were interruptions in the routine, the changes were usually directed by his captors. He had few worthwhile decisions to make.

For seven years, my friend dreamed of being released into a life of freedom. Finally, that moment came. Think of the joy of it. But also think of the readjustment that moving from captivity to freedom requires. I'm sure that as my friend sought to embrace his new and different life-style, there were times when he was plagued by anxiety and indecisiveness. There may have been moments when he wished for somebody else to make his decisions for him.

For more than seven years, I was a prisoner of the Not-OK Gospel. Upon obtaining my release, I found it difficult to cope with my newly acquired freedoms. Let me relate some of my struggles.

Communicating Myself Honestly

The free style of living which is afforded me by the OK Gospel permits me to communicate face to face with other persons. But what about those masks I've been wearing? I've grown to like them. One of them makes me look handsome. Others make me appear richer, wiser, more "Christian." When I take off my masks, I feel naked and exposed. Because I haven't liked myself, I can't relish the thought of projecting my real self to others. I don't even know for sure who I really am!

The first step toward an authentic communication of myself is to get to know myself — all aspects of my thinking, feeling, acting self. Not to know myself as I used to be or as I fondly think of myself being, but the person I really am. The second step is to express my understanding of myself to other persons honestly and clearly. Not as the player who improvises according to the cheers or boos of his audience, but as the actor who has the courage to project his own understanding of life and his own feelings.

A man and his wife got into an argument. Their faces reddened, their hands flailed the air, their voices snarled. Now, picture this: The telephone rings. The wife lifts the receiver to her ear and in a dulcet tone whispers, "Hel-l-lo." Why the change? *Audience!*

I walked into a general store where the air was blue with profanities which came boiling out of the proprietor's wife. "Honey," the proprietor said, nudging his wife, "this here gentleman's a preacher." *Audience!*

Sometimes we are unable or unwilling to communicate who we are to the other person frankly and honestly. A friend, a woman, said to me, "Ben, have I offended you in some way? Lately, you've been cool and distant."

Her direct question brought me face to face with the fact that I had not communicated well. Whenever she was near, I became keenly aware of her feminine appeal. Because my "parent" tapes began telling me, "That's bad," I was frightened. I felt trapped and I withdrew. But the message which *she* got was, "Something must be wrong with me because my friend is putting distance between us."

After becoming aware of my feelings and reactions, did I have the courage to tell her the truth? In this instance, I did.

"Sue," I said, "you've done nothing to offend me. Let me take this occasion to affirm that you are a very appealing person. I appreciate you and I value our friendship. Actually, what you've been picking up are vibrations from my own insecurity. You see, I don't know how to handle positive feelings toward someone of the opposite sex. Often, I try to deny these feelings, and if I fail, I seek to protect myself from awkwardness by appearing to be busy or preoccupied."

Honest communication took the weight of my not-OK feelings off my friend and enhanced our relationship.

In this episode, I was communicating at two levels. At first, I was using *words* to cover my real feelings, but my *nonverbal* communication gave me away — my nonverbal communication told her that something was wrong with our relationship. By "leveling" with her, I obtained sufficient release for my words and my nonverbal communication to be consistent with each other and with my intentions.

As I embrace a life-style of open honesty, I recognize that I want to adopt methods of open and honest communication. The OK Gospel tells me that the Christian faith is relational, embracing my relationships with God, with other persons, and with myself.

The stages through which I communicate with others are: (1) I come to an honest understanding of my feelings; (2) I express these feelings honestly and accurately (plus sensitively and lovingly) to the other person; and (3) I receive feedback which tells me that I either am accurately projecting myself and my sense of the relationship or I am failing to do so. If I am failing, I must make adjustments. These steps are essential to meaningful communication.

In sharp contrast with this process is the closed style of communication (in fact, it hardly deserves to be called "communication"). In each encounter, I intend to project my own values and I persist in this. As to feedback, I am too busy projecting to listen. Of course, if you affirm me, I will take cognizance of that. But if you oppose me, I will ignore your feedback, distort it, or try to drown it out.

The closed approach to communication cannot support and sustain a relational life-style; therefore, I reject it as a hindrance to my intention to be OK and to accept other persons as OK.

Living Flexibly with Roles

A closed style of living necessitates narrow experiences, and narrow experiences encourage me to see myself in a rigidly defined role. I see myself in terms of what my parents, family, community, and culture have expected of me. I feel most comfortable and expert in this narrow role, for it's the stance and style that I have practiced.

Society expects (or certainly did until recently) the *woman* to cook, wash, mend, scrub, decorate, entertain. Men don't cook meals or make up beds. I am a man; it follows that I do not cook. But I *like* to cook. Am I going to accept society's prescribed role, or am I going to feel free to engage in this activity, which I enjoy? Besides, I'm a *good* cook. You ought to taste some of the bread that I bake. The answer is, I'm not going to let the culture dictate role restrictions which are contradictory to my nature.

Similarly, the culture has made man the breadwinner. But now women are insisting that they have the opportunity to express themselves in jobs outside the home and to enjoy the satisfaction of contributing to their family's income. And I ask, when it's mutually agreed upon, why shouldn't the wife work? Such an outlet might improve the marital relationship. Perhaps there ought to be an alternation of roles. But there's the question: Can the husband free himself from society's image of men supporting their families and accept this reversal of roles?

Role reversal might also be helpful in the church. For a long period, I was so immersed in my clergyman role that I ate, slept, and talked nothing but "clergy." In this role-playing, I probably shut many laymen out; certainly, I closed myself off from many avenues to personal growth. Sometimes, persons responded to me as though I were a third sex. I think I would like a system in which clergymen and laymen would alternately minister to each other.

As an experiment, on the left side of a piece of paper, set down in a column the various roles that you fill: wife, mother, daughter, part-time secretary, club president, etc. Now, opposite each entry write the counterpart role. To match the hypothetical list above: husband, son/daughter, father/mother, boss, club member, etc. Now, imagine what it would be like to fill the role of each of your counterparts. Psychologically, could you shift into these roles without considerable trauma?

I must not equate my identity with either my role or my functions within a role. Again, as an experiment, start identifying yourself as a person rather than as a role. When someone introduces himself to you, say, "I'm Jane Jones, and I happen to be a housewife" — or "I'm also a housewife" — or "I function as a housewife." See how the other person will react and whether or not it will make a difference in how you view yourself.

Living with New Experiences

The not-OK person's closed life-stance causes him to be suspicious and fearful of change.

When the Revised Standard Version of the Bible appeared in 1952, it was feared and fought in many quarters. Some said that the translators had deliberately "watered down" the scriptures. Others said that the book was communist inspired. Some gave it the derogatory label of "The Communist Version." *Doesn't it have a red cover?*

Two decades ago, Harry Emerson Fosdick, pastor of Riverside Church in New York City and the dominant liberal of his era, was called names such as "apostle of the devil." Conservative leaders admonished preachers and laymen alike that they should shun both Dr. Fosdick and his writing.

In this decade, encounter groups have been labeled destroyers of values, substitutes for repentance, and a tool used by the communists to brainwash Christians.

These are manifestations of a closed life-style. An open life-style evaluates both the change and the change agent on the basis of their merits or lack of merit. We cling to the verities of our lives — the love of God, the presence of the Spirit, our kinship with our brothers — while venturing out to investigate new activities and new relationships. We do not accept everything new that comes down the pike, but we are open to its consideration instead of automatically yelping and fleeing in horror.

Now, twenty years later, most of us not only read the RSV with confidence, but we also use interpretations of the Bible which are frankly identified as "paraphrases." One of my favorites is *The Living Bible*. The interpreter, Ken Taylor, makes no pretense that this is a literal translation of the Greek or Hebrew. He acknowledges that it is his own elaboration. Accepting it in this light, I find it a valuable aid as I attempt to understand Christ's message to this age. Yet, even today Ken Taylor is rebuffed by persons who accuse him of tampering with the word of God.

When I finally got up the courage to read Harry Emerson Fosdick, I discovered to my amazement that he was no demonic character; rather, he was a sensitive, intelligent, deeply dedicated Christian. At a strategic point in my life, his autobiography, *The Living of These Days*, enabled me to loose some of the bonds of my past and to move more freely into the future. While I did not agree with all his ideas, Fosdick communicated the Spirit of Christ to me.

I recently attended a personal growth lab. The leader didn't brainwash me or destroy my values. Quite the opposite. The experience helped me to identify blocks to my growth.

As I grow more willing to open myself to experiences, I am much less frightened about the future. I experience the Spirit of God more frequently. Living is no longer a chore; it's an exciting adventure. Not only do I try to be receptive to new experiences; I also place myself in positions where new experiences might come along.

Right now, I would like to have encounters of dialogue with:

■ non-Christians who have no use for the church, for Christ, or my value system.

■ black persons who are revolutionary because they have not shared in the affluence of the nation.

■ youth who have rejected the system.

■ charismatic leaders who are helping to shape the renewal of the church.

■ homosexuals.

■ divorcees who are struggling to find meaning and direction in their lives.

■ radical political leaders.

When I functioned out of a closed system, I had no desire for these encounters. I would have been afraid to relate closely to persons who were so different. But now I find exchanges with new types to be entertaining and stimulating.

Living with Others as Equals

A closed style has the element of superiority (the pharisee dimension) built into it.

In a closed system, I believe that:

My point of view is exclusively correct.

Persons who think differently ought to be converted to my view. (I know what's best for them.)

By avoiding persons who disagree with me, I will protect myself from contamination and, at the same time, weaken their status.

From an open stance, I not only accept my worth before God; I also accept the worth of every other person. A man has value, not because of his attainment, but because he is a unique person created in the image of God. I want to help each person discover and express his uniqueness.

In our house church, we once came into serious and somewhat destructive conflict. Several in the congregation were adamant in asserting a certain interpretation of biblical teaching about the Christian family. Others felt that this interpretation was too narrow and negated other Christian values. After several exchanges — in which a few members were personally wounded — we designed a weekend conference to discuss the ways we wanted to relate to each other. After hours of discussion, we decided:

> Each of us will be responsible to each member of the congregation to enable him to discover his unique gifts; we will support him as he seeks to exercise those gifts; and we will give him our trust and love as he endeavors to live out his own life style.

This statement expresses open acceptance of others as equals, each with his own contribution to make.

Living Out of Trust

The OK person lives out of open trust. The not-OK person can also trust, but his is a "closed" trust. Closed trust is the affirmation of an established body of knowledge, or set of concepts, or collection of beliefs. In religion, this means to trust certain theological propositions. These propositions become the standards by which all of the content of spiritual and social conduct is formulated and out of which a life-style is determined.

Probe around under closed trust and you'll discover a pool of not-OK feelings. "God is OK, but I'm not." The not-OK person requires something solid and steady to cling to, and these religious propositions are about as rigid and unchanging as anything he can find. The not-OK person submits himself to these ready-made theological propositions although they may be illogical, may be humanly impossible to live up to, and may contradict his sense of his own being.

Let me illustrate. A man and a woman were discussing God's power to answer prayer. The man said, "If we pray in faith, God will answer our prayers."

The woman responded, "I prayed for the ill child of a friend and the child died."

The man answered, "Possibly you were praying in the wrong way. Maybe you did not exercise faith."

"But I used all the faith I had, and I expected God to answer my prayer!"

"God may have been trying to teach the parent something about his plan."

"Would he let four persons in her family die with the same disease to teach her something?"

"But God always answers prayer," the man urged, "and something is wrong with us if we do not receive his answers."

This man was clinging in blind faith to a proposition and the deductions flowing from it, although life experiences demonstrated that truth lay elsewhere. His blind faith demanded that he reject outright this questing Christian woman, who could not embrace his view because it ran counter to her own understanding of God, gained from the Bible and in her life experiences. (If we were to surrender absolutely to blind trust, then we would reject the whole message of the Bible, for it is essentially the story of man's discovering a truer picture of God and the God-man relationship — which is to say, the story of people who said, "I don't think that God is like that.")

There are propositions in open trust, too: God is; he loves; he acts in our lives; he answers prayer. But open trust has no rigid expectations of how these affirmations must appear in life. Open trust affirms that God answers prayers, but it feels no necessity to prove that God *always* answers prayers *as we desire him to*.

In my experience, open trust is based upon some broad principles which God has revealed in scripture, but it remains flexible and adaptive to each particular situation. In every life encounter, trust may have a different appearance. Whether I am experiencing sickness or health, loneliness or community, loss of friends or celebration, I must act out of open trust. My response to God has the possibility of many faces.

Living My Identity

For most of my life, I endeavored to achieve my identity by performance. I requested, "Tell me that I am *somebody* because I have performed successfully." For example:

"Mother, tell me I'm *somebody* because I have been obedient to you."

"Dad, tell me I'm *somebody* because I have made all A's on my report card."

"Teacher, tell me I'm *somebody* because I have answered the questions correctly."

"Wife, tell me I'm *somebody* because I have provided adequately for you and the children."

"Peers, tell me I'm *somebody* because I have achieved objectives which seemed impossible ten years ago."

I shifted from one image of myself to another. In succession, I was the dynamic young evangelist — dedicated pastor — good and faithful husband — loving father — Mr. Lay Witness Mission — and on and on. My disillusionments tell me that I am not, and cannot be, an assumed identity. I do not turn my dial to whatever image I choose and thereby find my identity. Instead, I tune in on who I am and let my image flow out of my understanding of myself. I live from the inside out, not the reverse.

In tuning in on myself, these questions are helpful·

1. What are my deepest feelings about myself, my life, and other persons?

2. What are my deepest desires and aspirations?

3. What are my values?

4. What physical, spiritual, and intellectual assets do I have?

5. What are my limitations?

6. What can I become on the basis of my interests, my assets, my limitations, and God's call?

When I obtain answers to questions like these and then live out of these answers, I am actualizing myself and my relationship with the Spirit.

Free-style living is applicable to every aspect of life, but in the next chapter, I want to look specifically at its application to marriage. Meanwhile, ponder this question: Would you say that in marriage we are inclined to be: (a) free and open? or (b) constrained and closed? Do you feel comfortable with — or threatened by — this question?

open letter to a bride

chapter 11

"I plan to marry Roman," our daughter announced.

"When?"

"Just as soon as possible."

Such an announcement seldom evokes enthusiasm from parents when the daughter is not quite eighteen. Certainly, an early marriage did not coincide with my expectations for Vange. After discussion and reflection, however, I saw that Vange did intend to marry Roman, and I could either join her or exclude myself from one of the most significant moments in her life — and mine. So I joined her to help her have the most meaningful wedding possible.

"Daddy, I don't want a wedding like everyone else's," Vange said. "I want a special ceremony, and I want you to conduct it. I also want a contemporary setting."

"What will that look like?"

"I don't know, but let's think about it together."

This request for help was significant. This was my daughter, and her wedding was the most important that I had helped to plan. Vange and I spent many hours talking about the form and content of the ceremony. Our planning drew us together. We were also gratified by Roman's approval as we shared our ideas with him.

On the day of the wedding, the caterer had the patio beautifully arranged. There were gorgeously decorated tables laden with cake and punch. A dozen potted plants brightened the yard. A friend had built a small platform in the back yard, and atop this we had placed a gazebo (a man-sized bird cage). Inside, hanging from the center, was a bouquet.

There had been one problem. At 10 a.m., the folding chairs had not arrived. It turned out that the area manager of the rental agency was filling in for the local manager, who had left a day early on vacation.

"I'm sorry," the manager said, "but somehow we overlooked your order. I'll try to get your chairs out to you, but I can't promise."

"Do you have a truck available?" I asked.

"Yes."

"Then I'll be there in fifteen minutes and haul the chairs myself."

By the time that our 200 guests arrived, no one could have suspected the sweat we'd been in. The back yard was carpeted with green grass and screened by trees. Birds chirped. And the one large bouquet hanging in the gazebo called attention to the spot where the ceremony would take place.

There was no music. Roman and his parents walked in first and sat on the right; then Vange, Betty, and I walked in and sat on the left. Walter Albritton, a very dear friend, greeted the guests and offered a prayer. Then I stood to conduct the rest of the ceremony, which focused on relationship based on love instead of loyalty based on rules.

The ceremony symbolized a free-style marriage:

A Contemporary Wedding Ceremony

Opening prayer.

Words of greeting.

There are two moments of unparalleled joy in the hearts of parents: the birth of a child and the marriage of that child.

The spirit of wedding is one of joy, gratitude, and expectation. It is a festive occasion to be celebrated and long remembered.

Long ago, God declared that it was not good for man to be alone, so he made woman and ordained the union of these two creatures of his. Persons in all nations through the ages have participated in this loving union of thoughts, feelings, and bodies.

For twenty centuries, we in the western world have recalled that this institution was blessed by Christ through his presence in Cana of Galilee, and today we respectfully request his presence to be here to make sacred the marriage of these two persons who have decided to commit themselves to each other in a partnership — for love, for mutual fulfillment, and a united search for the meaning of their lives.

Truly, this is a festive occasion. We parents are grateful that you have chosen to celebrate with us the marriage of our children, Vange and Roman.

Statement of desire.

Roman, will you today take Vange as your wife?
Will you love her?
Will you trust her?
Will you be loyal to her?
Will you be honest with her?

And will you endeavor to achieve a relationship in which both your needs and hers may be met in all the circumstances of life through which you pass . . .

Whether it is sickness or health, poverty or wealth, joy or pain?

Roman: I will.

Vange, will you today take Roman as your husband?
Will you love him?
Will you trust him?
Will you be loyal to him?
Will you be honest with him?
And will you endeavor to achieve a relationship in which both your needs and his may be met in all the circumstances of life through which you pass . . .

Whether it is sickness or health, poverty or wealth, joy or pain?

Vange: I will.

Roman and Vange, since you have made the decision to unite your hearts in a quest for life's meaning together, I now ask you before God and this community of faith to make public your choice of and your commitment to each other.

Roman, from his heart: Vange, I love you; I trust you; I will be loyal to you; I will be honest with you; and I will endeavor to achieve a relationship with you in which love, trust, loyalty, and honesty may prevail and that together we may discover the meaning of our lives.

Vange, from her heart: Roman, I love you; I trust you; I will be loyal to you; I will be honest with you; and I will endeavor to achieve a relationship with you in which love, trust, loyalty, and honesty may prevail and that together we may discover the meaning of our lives.

Quotation from Gibran's "The Prophet"

Many times, the question has been asked: "What is marriage?"

Ancient Wisdom answers:

"You were born together, and together you shall be forevermore.

You shall be together when the white wings of death scatter your days.

Aye, you shall be together even in the silent memory of God.

But let there be spaces in your togetherness,

And let the winds of the heavens dance between you.

"Love one another, but make not a bond of love:

Let it rather be a moving sea between the shores of your souls.

Fill each other's cup but drink not from one cup.

Give one another of your bread but eat not from the same loaf.

Sing and dance together and be joyous, but let each one of you be alone,

Even as the strings of a lute are alone though they quiver with the same music.

"Give your hearts, but not into each other's keeping.

For only the hand of Life can contain your hearts.

And stand together yet not too near together:

For the pillars of the temple stand apart,

And the oak tree and the cypress grow not in each other's shadow."[6]

The Ring Ceremony.

This ring is an outward and visible symbol of the love and trust, loyalty and honesty which you feel in your hearts. And it is a tangible representation of the commitment you are making to each other.

Roman: Vange, I give you this ring as a symbol of the love I feel in my heart and the commitment of myself to you. May our love grow as long as we both shall live.

Vange: Roman, I give you this ring as a symbol of the love I feel in my heart and the commitment of myself to you. May our love grow as long as we both shall live.

Pronouncement.

Dear friends, together we have witnessed this man and this woman state their desire to be united in marriage: to love; to trust; to be loyal; to be honest; and to seek a deep and abiding relationship with each other.

We have heard the vows which they have sincerely stated to one another. We further have witnessed their love and commitment through the giving and receiving of rings.

Now, Vange and Roman, I believe God is pleased for you to be united in marriage.

To learn the meaning of love . . . in joy and in sorrow . . . in sickness and in health . . . in success and in failure . . . and in all the stages of growth and change through which you will pass together.

So, by the authority given me in the Church of Jesus Christ our Lord, I now pronounce that you are husband and wife together.

In the name of the Father, and the Son, and the Holy Spirit.

Prayer.

Thank you, God, for the day of Roman's and Vange's birth. Thank you for this day on which they have made public their decision to join their lives together in love.

I pray that you will be in their lives . . . to guide them . . . to instruct them . . . to enable them together to become the persons that you destined them to be . . .

And I ask you to be in their lives as they lay the foundation for a loving home.

Help us in this community to accept them . . . affirm them . . . and support them . . . as they establish a home together. We ask through Jesus Christ our Lord, who taught us to pray . . .

> *Our Father which art in heaven, Hallowed be*
> *thy name.*
> *Thy kingdom come. Thy will be done in earth,*
> *as it is in heaven.*
> *Give us this day our daily bread.*

*And forgive us our debts, as we forgive our
debtors.
And lead us not into temptation, but deliver
us from evil: For thine is the kingdom, and
the power, and the glory, for ever. Amen.*
(Matt. 6:9-13 KJV)

Note the elements of this ceremony which Vange and I
composed. The ceremony exemplifies the open life-style we
have been discussing in this book. First, it takes both the
man and the woman seriously; each is a person independent
of the other. Second, it asks them to come together as independent human beings and unite their lives in a complementary way. Third, it underscores honesty and openness
as the way to build a meaningful relationship. Fourth, it
recognizes that both persons have needs as they come into
the marriage and that each is committed to helping the other
in meeting these needs.[7]

The events leading up to the wedding provided opportunities for the budding of the communal aspect of marriage. For
example, one evening before the wedding, the Krampls came
over for cake and coffee. We reviewed the ceremony and
Victor said, "Ben, you and Vange have certainly written a
fine ceremony and I hope that Roman and Vange will be able
to fulfill all those things which they are saying to one
another."

As the two families shared their hopes for this marriage
that evening, Vange's and Roman's larger community began
forming. Vange was experiencing her in-laws in a new setting
with us, and Roman was experiencing his relation with Vange
in the presence of his parents and Vange's.

The 200 persons who filled our back yard on the evening
of the wedding represented several significant communities.
Some were members of our spiritual community — our
house church and our lay renewal work. Another segment
consisted of old friends of both families. Still another group
came from our immediate neighborhood. Then, too, there
were colleagues from our places of work. All these persons
represented the larger community with which Roman and

Vange were identifying themselves. Finally, there were young friends in mod dress and with plenty of hair. These represented Vange's and Roman's peer group.

When the final "Amen" had been uttered, I stepped from the gazebo and said:

"Vange and Roman today have made a decision to unite their lives together in marriage. Each of you has come to celebrate this occasion with them. At this time, I am asking Victor and Anna Krampl to come and welcome Vange into their family, and Betty and I will welcome Roman into our family.

"Then, I want you, our friends, who represent the larger communities of church, neighborhood, and friendship, to come forward and welcome this couple into these larger communities."

For the next hour or so, these communities reached out their hands, symbolically and physically, and welcomed Vange and Roman into their world. This fellowship, I said to myself, is certainly a gift of the Spirit. The warmth of these friends and my awareness of God's presence caused me to feel that my earlier misgivings were wasted worry. I feel confident that each September first, Vange and Roman will fondly recall the love and affirmation which were offered to them on their wedding day.

I invite you to sit in as I share with Roman and Vange the implications of their ceremony for an open, free, authentic marriage.

"To both of you I would like to say:

"*Bring a number of past experiences into this relationship, but place them in the new perspective.* For example, Vange, you *could* react to Roman as you have to me and he *could* fall into the trap of responding to you as he did to his parents, but you will have a better relationship if you live in the here and now, relating to each other realistically in the present situation.

"I do not know the expectations which each of you is bringing into this relationship. Possibly you cannot articulate these to yourself today; it is equally likely that you do have some pretty deep feelings about your hopes. *Be realistic in your expectations.* Not all of your needs will be met through this relationship. Don't place a greater burden on the other person than he or she can carry. If your expectations are too high, you are setting the stage for a great deal of disappointment and consequent pain in your lives. Share openly your hopes and dreams, but permit them to be reshaped by the other's response.

"*Spend a lot of time together.* Love each other. Experience each other in every way, but remember the wise words that you requested from Gibran:

> But let there be spaces in your togetherness,
> And let the winds of the heavens dance between you.
> Love one another, but make not a bond of love. . .[8]

"If you keep some space in your relationship, you will preserve your unique identities and bring more strength and love to each other than you could if you permit your lives to become symbiotic.

"*Don't allow yourself to get hung up in a rigid role.* I mean, don't think of yourself primarily as a 'housekeeper,' or a 'breadwinner,' or whatever. Be *persons*. Likewise, try not to impose a role on your mate — let each be his own person. Help each other to be who he is and keep on appreciating him for it. Remain flexible in your own role and permit the other person to change also when the change will enable a fuller expression of his being.

"*Negotiate a clear, workable contract between you.* I hope that you both will develop broad relationships outside your marriage. As you relate deeply to other persons, you will be enriched and you can bring this new breadth into your relationship with each other, and both of you will be enlarged by it. If you seek to control and monopolize each other, you will become bitter. If you do not give each other the freedom for other significant relationships, you will stifle your opportunities for spontaneity in your sharing together.

"*Look upon yourselves as equals.* There will be certain aspects of your relationship where one of you will bring the greater strength, but don't flaunt your strength so that your mate feels insecure; rather, share your strength so that you both may be strong. Likewise, discover where your partner's strengths offset some of your weaknesses and freely receive his support. I have seen you already functioning like this, and I hope you will continue.

"*You each have a unique identity within yourself.* No person can give you identity; you must *be* your identity. Many of us mistakenly try to get our identity from our spouse. This effort is certain to fail.

"*I hope that you will be open to new experiences* in yourselves, in your relationship together, and in your other life relationships. These relationships will come to you; accept them and enjoy them.

"*Hold steady when change occurs.* Even the most secure person can be frightened by unexpected change, but the more you learn to accept the inevitability of change, the better prepared you will be. You will not always feel as you do today. Your strength will come from new places. As both of you grow, prepare for your relationship to change and grow, too.

"*I hope you will discover the meaning and the power of trust.* I think learning to trust yourself will be your most difficult task — it has been hard for me. I hope you will also have a deep trust in each other; if you let your belief in your mate be stronger than any struggle which he faces, he will draw strength from your confidence.

"The source of lasting trust is God. God is the foundation of your life and he is with you in your efforts to become a whole, mature person as he is with you in your desire to establish a happy and lasting home. I do not know what shape your encounter with God will take; I do not know how you will respond to him individually or together. I am confident that at the proper time and in a very significant way, his presence will be revealed to you.

"*Finally, this word to you, Vange. Your life has unlimited possibilities.* I believe this. I have always believed it. You did not choose the path that I had dreamed of for you. I had planned on your going to college, studying music, and developing certain unique potentials which I have observed in you. I have no lasting regrets about your decision to marry Roman at this time rather than to go to college. You have every right to be your own person and to live your own life. Today, I encourage you to get in touch with your deepest desires and to set in motion plans to become the person that God destines you to be. *You are a unique, unrepeatable miracle of God.*"

I believe that the words which I have written to Vange and Roman apply to me, to you, and to others. I have written them out of a background of both painful and joyous experiences.

A free, open marriage is a worthy goal, but it has little chance to succeed unless the couple practices good communication. In the next chapter, I want to look with you at some principles for improving family communication.

when family connections break
chapter 12

"There has never been a more beautiful bride," a friend said to me on Vange's and Roman's wedding day.

I enthusiastically agreed. *I was her father!* Fathers are

easily smitten by their daughters. But don't *most* girls show their best charm and beauty on their wedding days? Why is this so?

I believe that brides are radiant because they are full of expectations. They have dreamed of a happy and fulfilling marriage, and, almost suddenly, their wedding day arrives. Will the marriage be all that the girl hopes it will be — or will it be predominantly frustration and disappointment? Whatever qualms the bride had during her courtship, she now pushes aside. This is as it should be. But the girl's parents may not be able to banish entirely the invading realization that "as long as you both shall live" can be a long, long time.

So much depends upon the expectations that the bride and the groom bring into the marriage; how well each expresses his expectations; how well each listens to (and senses) the other's expectations, and how well their expectations are either realized or reshaped through the growing process.

If you are married or have been married, consider your own experience. What expectations did you bring to your marriage?

Have they been met?

Have they been crushed?

Or, do you still have hopes that they will be met?

A couple, friends of mine, attended a conference at Laity Lodge while Keith Miller was director. One evening, Keith asked each couple to retire to their room. For a thirty-minute period, first the one and then the other spouse was to state the expectations which he/she brought into the marriage. As each spoke, the other was to listen, without interruption, and then feed back his understanding of what had been shared. My friends said that this simple exercise exposed the primary source of the hostility which they felt: *frustrated expectations.*

Undoubtedly, one of the factors deciding whether a marriage will consummate expectations or negate expectations is the quality of communication. Dreams must be stated clearly, not disguised. Dreams must be heard honestly and sympathetically, not ignored, distorted, or minimized.

For an example of relationship-blocking communication (or lack of communication), I invite you to come along for a visit with the Jamison family. It's Tuesday evening and the Jamisons have just finished dinner.

James Jamison controls a successful carpet company. Mary, his wife, is a graduate of a private woman's college in Virginia. Bill is a high-school senior, and Susan is a high-school freshman. The topic of their "routine chat" is summer vacation.

Jim (1): Mary, why haven't you brought the travel guides down from the attic? You know we can't make any decent decisions without adequate information.

Mary (1): I'm so sorry, Honey, I just haven't had time today. I feel so bad because I never seem to have things prepared for our family conference time.

Jim (2): If you would become more organized, maybe this household would run smoother. Instead, you yak on the phone all day and the really important things in our family life go unattended.

Bill (1): Say, dad, didn't we have a lot of fun last summer at the beach? Remember trying to sail those two-man boats in the Gulf?

Jim (3): Yeah. Good fun. But maybe if you helped your mother with the household chores, she could have got out the guide books.

Sue (1): Guess what I made on my spelling test today.

Mary (2): Now, Jim, you know how hard it is for us to get all the pieces together for our planning. Just be patient.

Jim (4): Patient, hell! I am sick and tired of working myself to death, coming home to incompetence, and being told to "be patient."

Mary (3): Get off your high horse, Jim. You're not at the office. I'm not your secretary and the kids are not office boys. You are so overcome with your sense of importance at the office you don't treat us like persons when you get home.

Sue (2): Martha and I are planning to go to the movie Saturday afternoon.

Bill (2): A few days ago I was reading an article in the

Reader's Digest about family vacations. This article pointed out that successful family vacations included all the members of the family in the planning.

Mary (4): What do you think we're trying to do tonight, Bill? If you didn't spend so much time reading magazines and spent a little more time helping me with house chores, the planning would get along smoothly.

Jim (5): Now, Mary, don't be too hard on Bill. I did come home rather ruffled. You know how hard I work and how thoughtless I can be of you and the children when I'm tired.

Sue (3): I think I left my gym shoes over at Marilyn's.

Bill (3): The persons who have successful vacations not only plan well, they also ensure variety in their vacations — at least, that's what the article said.

How far do you suppose the Jamison family proceeded with planning their summer vacation? And even if they managed to select an ideal place, do you think you would have enjoyed going with them? I wonder what Jim and Mary expected from their marriage, and how they see those expectations now. If they are unable to discuss a relatively "safe" subject like vacation, it's likely neither would dare disclose his secret longings.

What's the trouble with the Jamisons?

For whatever reasons, the Jamisons aren't connecting with each other. It appears that each one lives behind a steel grating — although he makes sounds and movements, he doesn't connect with anyone else.

How many of us have suffered the same pain in the families in which we grew up — or, perhaps, in the family in which we live today?

Let's go back and analyze the transactions which took place in the family conference:

Jim (1) begins by blaming Mary. Whatever he was feeling inside (for example, anger over an unresolved dispute at the office), he has screened.

Mary (1) tries to appease Jim's anger by placating. She probably feels guilty and frightened.

Bill (1) endeavors to make peace between his parents by

intellectualizing about something pleasant. He feels frightened when his parents disagree.

Jim (3) attacks Bill without noting the intent of Bill's statement.

Sue (1) feels uncomfortable and brings up an irrelevant idea.

Mary (2) and Jim (4) play their game in reverse.

Mary (3) changes roles with Jim and becomes a blamer.

Sue (2) makes another irrelevant statement.

Bill (2), after being blasted by his father for his first entry into the conversation, seeks safety by hiding behind an authority — the *Reader's Digest* article.

Mary (4) feels stronger when she's angry, so now she attacks Bill.

Jim (5) becomes an appeaser between his wife and son and seeks to placate his wife.

Obviously, these transactions could continue indefinitely without the family ever dealing seriously and honestly with the subject at hand. More importantly, these persons' lives will not touch each other as long as they communicate in these painful and ineffective ways. The suffering resulting from such encounters will drive each member to a safer distance from the others. The inevitable result is disintegration. A household must necessarily be a place where its members feel free to share secret longings and where conversation builds as it goes rather than destructs.

I am indebted to Virginia Satir for some valuable tools which I use to analyze barriers to communication.[9] She identifies four blocks to conversation, and she terms these *placating, blaming, intellectualizing,* and *distracting.*

In the Jamison episode Jim is a *blamer,* his wife a *placater,* his son an *intellectualizer,* and his daughter a *distracter.* At one point in the dialogue, Jim and his wife exchange roles.

Let me define each block and describe its posture, the feelings that accompany it, and the ensuing results.

First, *placating.* I myself have been a placater. As a placater, my words are, "Whatever you want is all right with me. I just want to make you happy." But in disguising my *true* feelings, I sense that I am on my knees begging for acceptance. On the inside, I am feeling like a zero, nothing! Sometimes I feel that if this person whom I am entreating rejects me, I am dead.

One evening, I was late for supper. My wife had grown tired of waiting and had eaten alone. She expressed her resentment over my being late, which caused me to feel guilty.

"I had wanted to go shopping this evening," she said.

I was hungry — and I hate shopping with a passion, but without hesitation, I approved. "Why don't we go! I'd love to go shopping with you."

We went. After Betty had tried on the fourth dress, I said, "Why don't you make up your mind? I like the last one you selected."

"Why did you decide to come shopping with me? You and I both know you don't like to shop."

With this confrontation, I was faced with a choice of either admitting I had placated Betty or blaming her for imposing on me. Within my experience, placating never works; the disguised feelings will eventually break out in a painful way.

Blaming, like placating, always blocks interpersonal relationships. The blamer assumes a posture of being taller than the other person. He is Gulliver looking down upon all the tiny Lilliputians. He is right, and the other person is wrong. If the blamer speaks loudly enough, he may blow people out of his way. A typical blamer says, "You never do anything the right way." Or, "What's wrong with you?"

For all his bluster, the blamer is basically insecure. On the inside, he feels lonely and afraid. ("I am shouting because I'm uncertain of myself, but if I take the offensive, maybe they won't discover my weakness.")

Blaming evokes anxiety, causing defenses to be erected. I recall arriving at the airport terminal and waiting on the upper level for Betty to pick me up. I had specified the time, allowing fifteen minutes to deplane and make my way to the curb in front of the terminal building.

I waited fifteen minutes and went downstairs to look for her. Just as I arrived, she passed. After one more circle, she pulled up — twenty-five minutes after the agreed-upon time.

"Why weren't you here when we agreed? You know I hate to wait at the airport."

"I've been here for thirty minutes; where have you been?" she responded.

"Upstairs, where I told you."

"You didn't tell me to meet you on the departing ramp. You were *arriving*, weren't you? I have been down here where I always meet you."

This blaming of each other could have continued indefinitely. One of us would have recalled another offense, like, "Well, remember that time when you didn't meet me at the grocery store as you said you would?"

Blaming evokes defensiveness — which brings more blaming — which triggers counter-blaming. It's a vicious cycle.

Now let's look at a combination of placating with blaming.

Husband: Let's go out to dinner this evening.

Wife: Okay, honey, whatever you would like to do. I just want to do the thing that will make you happy.

Husband: Where do you want to go?

Wife: Oh, anywhere at all. Wherever you like.

(They enter his favorite restaurant.)

Husband: Here we are at the Brass Plate. I really hope you enjoy your dinner.

Wife: Why did you choose this restaurant? You know I don't like the Brass Plate. They don't have a good seafood selection here.

Husband: Why didn't you tell me where you wanted to go? *Another evening ruined!*

First, the husband begins with good motives. The wife placates, then later blames her husband for a poor choice. Finally, he blames her for not speaking up. The entire episode models the devastating effect of poor communication between mates.

Intellectualizing is just as deadly as placating or blaming. The intellectualizer appears to be very reasonable. Often, he speaks in the third person. For example: "If one would pay attention to both one's spending and one's bank balance, he probably would not overdraw his account." While the intellectualizer appears cool, calm, and collected, on the inside he is frightened. He feels vulnerable, but he pridefully represses his feelings of weakness.

Here's an example of intellectualizing:

Wife: I'm worried about some of the kids Susie's running around with.

Husband: What's wrong with them?

Wife: Nothing specifically. I just feel uneasy.

Husband: One should not hunt for trouble. And I don't think it's good for parents to make hasty judgments about their children's companions. The McCarthy hearings demonstrated that the old saying that "birds of a feather flock together" is an unfair proposition, and an invasion of one's individual rights, as well.

In this illustration, the husband failed to sense his wife's feelings. She wasn't indicting her daughter; she wasn't even recommending that the daughter be barred from seeing these friends. She was concerned, and her husband could have helped her to resolve this concern.

There's a difference between being *intellectual* and *intellectualizing.* A professor can be an intelligent resource person for his students. But he will never build relationships if he intellectualizes and hides behind data to shield his opinions and feelings. Data doesn't relate; persons relate! If I'm to relate, I have to make myself vulnerable; I can't hide behind intellectualizing.

Finally, there is the *distracting* mode. Here the words are irrelevant to whatever else is being said. The irrelevant person reminds me of a tightrope-walker who is struggling to keep from falling off on either side. "There is no place for me in this conversation," he says. "Nobody here cares what I have to say, anyway." Whether he intends it or not, such a person blocks serious conversation.

A personal-growth group was role playing these four stances. The subject was planning for a trip. I recall that the person playing the distractor said, "I left my shoes at the movie." Her response was so disconnected that the group erupted in laughter. Since then, I have been plagued by distracters on a number of occasions, and I have wished I could obtain the same sort of instant relief.

While I believe that these four blocks destroy communication, there is one barrier which is more deadly — *withdrawal*. Even the blamer or the placater is making some effort to communicate with another person, but the person who withdraws closes out all opportunity for communication.

There are times when withdrawal is needed. It is important, however, that the need for withdrawal and the reasons behind the need be communicated to the other person. Earlier, I recommended that when negative feelings begin swirling inside you and you can't identify them or sort them out, you say to the other person, "I'm not sure just how I feel about this situation, but if you'll give me a little time, I'll try to respond." An abrupt, unexplained withdrawal ruptures communication, but a negotiated withdrawal preserves the lines of communication.

Communication is blocked by the five barriers which we have examined here. On the other hand, communication is facilitated by honesty and clarity. Some of us aren't living up to our communications potential, and we're going to have to discard our old styles and adopt new styles. For me, four essentials apply: (1) stating clearly and honestly what is going on with me; (2) receiving feedback; (3) listening in depth to those who are seeking to communicate with me; and (4) enabling others to search deeper into themselves.

Recently I was conducting a workshop on communication skills. After the participants had completed a personal inventory which put them in touch with feelings about themselves, their values, their sense of accomplishments, and their problem areas, I asked them to arrange themselves in groups of four. I then assigned each of them a function.

Let me describe these functions. Assume that the four persons are seated north, south, east, and west. To begin the communication, I asked North to be the *Revealer*. His task was to state clearly to the other three persons what specific experiences he had recalled in filling out his personal inventory. He was to describe fully and candidly his feelings about each event.

South was to be the *Reflector*. He was to reflect back to the Revealer the content of what he heard the Revealer saying. He was to report, not interpret.

West was the *Responder*. This is an interpretative role. The Responder tries to draw from the Revealer's words and nonverbal expressions the true picture of the Revealer's feelings. He relates the Revealer's experience and feelings to similar circumstances in his own life and responds to the Revealer by sharing this part of himself.

East was the *Researcher*. He poses questions or makes suggestions which may enable the Revealer to look more deeply and more honestly into his feelings. I urged the Researcher to use questions which begin with "What" or "How" rather than to employ "Why" questions because "Why?" tends to put persons on the defensive. If a person is forced to justify his feelings, he may not reveal his feelings and thereby become vulnerable.

I had the foursomes switch roles until each person had the opportunity to be Revealer, Reflector, Responder, and Researcher.

In any interpersonal communication, these four functions are operating. For any real communication to take place, someone must be. willing to reveal himself. Feedback is necessary if he is to be sure that his message is getting through. And he needs reflective questions ("You felt angry, didn't you?") and supportive statements ("I know how you felt because I had someone say that I was a monotone, also.").

(It's interesting to note that when a person tries to thrash out an issue by himself, he may play each of the roles involved in the game which I directed.)

But to come back to the family relationship. Consider the five negative mechanisms — blaming, placating, intellectualizing, distracting, and withdrawal — over against the devices of revealing, reflecting, responding, and researching.

Consider how these four "R's" might have helped the Jamisons.

Jim: Man, did I have a hard day at the plant. A breakdown shut down one line for five hours.

Mary: I know how you feel. It's been a frustrating day for me, too. I meant to get our travel guides down so we could better plan our vacation.

Bill: I guess you feel like selling out and quitting, huh, Dad?

Sue: But we appreciate your working and earning money so we can go on a vacation.

Jim: Well, there's nothing like having a family to cheer you.

Mary: Do you think we'd enjoy going back to that Gulf resort, Jim? We all seemed to enjoy it last year.

Bill: Those two-man boats were peachy keen.

Jim: That might be nice, but why don't we defer a decision until we have a chance to get those guides down from the attic. I'm afraid I'm too tired and uptight to think clearly tonight.

As you try to improve your communications with your family, try these four "R's." Permit yourself to reveal yourself even if to do so makes you feel uneasy. Ask other members of the family what they think about your situation. If the communicating begins to drag or turn negative, shift into the role of reflecting, responding, or researching — or all three.

Remember, don't give up just because one or two attempts at improved communication fail. Improvement requires effort and time, practice and patience.

Any worthwhile relationship is founded on high, but reasonable, expectations. But expectations are of no value unless they are communicated, for how else can they be affirmed or reshaped? *How else can they be lived?*

118

the search
for a church

chapter 13

I am a unique, unrepeatable miracle of God, and I need a spiritual community in which I can celebrate this gift. I need a fellowship in which I can share experiences of the Spirit, express my feelings, and affirm other persons. The need for this kind of supportive community grows especially acute whenever I confront hard-to-change patterns and dare to venture outside my old, protective self and into a new, free style of living.

When I was converted to Christ, I was given the impression that the church which I was joining was that kind of fellowship. It didn't meet this expectation. I've been hearing the same promise ever since, and I've repeatedly been disappointed. Many church leaders have told me that I haven't done enough, given enough, or cooperated enough to capture the prize, and perhaps this has at times been true.

But consider some of the conditions that are imposed:

if I attend all its meetings;
if I affirm all its actions;
if I have no ideas of my own;
if I do not try to change it;
if I support its leaders;
if I do not question its motives in trying to preserve itself.

In short, *if* I remain a child in faith and permit the church to be the parent, then and only then will the church accept me.

It took me fifteen years to recognize what the institution that I called "the church" was doing to me. Not until I came out of the pulpit, yet sought to continue to be a loyal worshiper, did I begin to recognize the emptiness of the traditional church experience. My position as a minister in the center of things hypnotized me into thinking that everyone was thriving in the glow of my pastoring. For me to come down out of the pulpit and sit in a pew was quite a letdown. As I repeatedly tried to overcome my reluctance to attend the Sunday service, I started having strange experiences.

I recall lying in bed one Sunday morning wondering, "What good excuse can I offer myself for not going to church? As a Christian, I ought to attend the services of the church faithfully and regularly — that's what I told hundreds of my parishioners. Don't all good Christians go to church on Sunday?"

But I knew down deep that I really didn't want to go. Why? I finally got up the courage to acknowledge what I had long suspected: I didn't want to go because the church didn't meet my needs. I felt that it was failing me in the following ways:

The style of leadership is authoritarian and clergy-centered. The minister is at stage center and the rest of the church focuses on him. Sure, the church often meets *his* needs — I knew this, for it had met mine.

I cannot truly participate in the worship experience. I am weary of the one-way, minister-to-me communication. There is no opportunity for me to confront his ideas with my own or to hear the thoughts of other persons around me.

I have experienced the new life of the Spirit of God and find it exciting and challenging, but *the structures of my church don't strengthen my personhood or fill my special needs.*

The church seems to be preoccupied with its own life. It seems to be telling me what I can do to preserve the church, not what I can do to fulfill my own dreams for myself, the Kingdom of God, and the world.

The church asks me to carry out its programs, which seem to originate "out there" somewhere. *The programs do not arise out of the needs of the people.* Programs which affect persons I have never seen in places I have never been seem to hold more romance for the church than programs which would deal directly with the reality of my own situation.

The church has a rule of precedent for almost every issue that arises. These legalisms preserve the past, with its appurtenant values and customs. At times, the church seems unaware that the Spirit of God can do *new* things among us.

All this adds up to my going to church carrying low expectations and coming away with them confirmed. The congregations in which I participated never seemed to believe that each person is a unique, unrepeatable miracle of God, with limitless potential. No wonder, then, that such a church never asks, "How can this church — this expression of the Body of Christ — enable *you* to become what God is calling you to be?"

In June, 1969, I boarded a plane in Jackson, Mississippi, to return to Atlanta from a vacation. The concerns which I've outlined here were buzzing around in my head. I pulled out my journal and wrote a question: "God, what do you want me to do?"

And the answer came:

"Begin an experimental church."

Even though my frustration had already convinced me that I had to find a new spiritual community, the experimental church suggestion evoked enormous fear within me. I wondered whether my own motives would be understood.

As soon as I arrived in Atlanta, I called a friend who had shared in the development of many of my ideas. His listening enabled me to conceptualize the idea concretely so that I could better evaluate it. As we talked, I realized that I was expressing authentically a deep part of my being. I felt the action of the Spirit of God. The next day, I talked with other friends and they endorsed the house church concept. It was as though the Spirit was rubber-stamping "Approved" on each idea as it emerged.

I consulted with a professor-friend whose doctrine of the church was conservative and institutional. I was surprised when he said, "I believe that you should undertake this experiment with a test congregation." I had expected a discourse on loyalty to existing forms. A long-time friend and national leader of my denomination came to Atlanta and I shared my concept with him. I expected him to be cautious, but his response was, "If you feel that this is what you need to do, I expect you had better get on with it."

With the encouragement of these friends, I began a systematic approach to the hierarchy of the United Methodist Church:

. the district superintendent,
. the resident bishop, and
. the bishop's cabinet.

A series of interviews culminated in the designation of a committee of four district superintendents to give direction to the initial stages of the experimental congregation.

The following projection was presented:

A PROPOSAL TO THE NORTH GEORGIA CONFERENCE OF THE UNITED METHODIST CHURCH

A SYNOPSIS OF THE SITUATION

1. The Church exists in a revolutionary culture, which has social, economic, racial, and political dimensions.

2. The present revolution is calling into question all of the established structures of our society, such as politics, education, and economics. The Christian Church is not exempt from this critical re-evaluation; neither is the United Methodist Church.

3. In a rapidly changing cultural situation, there is a radical demand for relevance on the part of the Church. At this point, it seems apparent that the Church is struggling to express itself with relevance.

4. Since there is a lack of clear models for the future, it is advisable to establish test models to discover new forms of the Church in the emerging culture.

BASIC COMMITMENTS FOR A TEST CONGREGATION

1. A Test Congregation, or an Experimental Congregation, must be committed to the historical church; that is, it must stand in continuity with the Church Catholic.

2. A Test Congregation must understand itself essentially as a fellowship of persons in Christ.

3. A Test Congregation must realize that its fellowship in Christ is sustained by both Word and Sacrament.

4. A Test Congregation will recognize itself as Laos, the People of God, with a shared ministry.

5. A Test Congregation must discover and affirm a discipline which is appropriate for the modern world. This discipline will include study and personal growth as well as the stewardship of material goods.

6. A Test Congregation must have a missional stance with explicit implications for involvement in the social structure.

RATIONALE FOR DEVELOPING A TEST CONGREGATION

1. The essence of the Church, which is a fellowship of persons in Jesus Christ, sustained by Word and Sacrament, is unchanging. It remains the same through history. The functions of the Church, such as evangelism, education, and mission, grow out of the Church's essential nature.

2. Whereas the essence and the functions which grow out of this essence of the Church do not change, the form (or structure) in which these functions express themselves must change. Forms (or structures) of the congregation must be appropriate for the culture and the situation in which the Church exists. The question, therefore, becomes: "What shape shall the Church take?" What is the most appropriate structure for any given period in history?

3. In response to these questions, idealism is helpful, but inadequate. The only adequate answer must include a tested, practical expression of the Church.

4. If the United Methodist Church is seriously seeking relevant forms of ministry and appropriate styles, it seems advisable to establish Test Congregations which can experiment with these forms.

5. In the event that a Test Congregation does discover new forms which are appropriate for the entire Church, these may be communicated through the existing structure of the Church to bring about gradual and creative change.

THE LIFE-STYLE OF A TEST CONGREGATION

1. The projected Test Congregation will be dedicated to a dialectical form of renewal. Dialectical renewal stands in contrast to a radical or revolutionary form of renewal. Whereas the latter seeks to abolish the existing structures of the Church with the intent to begin anew, dialectical renewal seeks to inject new life into existing structures. While new life initiates change in old structures, existing structures both condition and contain the new life.

2. In an era of ecumenicity, it is important that a Test Congregation discover grass-roots forms of the Ecumenical Church.

3. An experimental congregation does not stand in judgment on the Institutional Church, but rather seeks to test structures of the existing Church, thereby affirming these structures, or discovering alternate forms which might prove more effective. A Test Congregation may examine forms such as:
   (a) Missionary giving.
   (b) Investment in land and buildings.
   (c) Possibility of a mobile congregation or house church congregation.

(d) Education in family groups versus education by age group.

(e) Participative forms of worship.

(f) The autocratic decision-making process versus decision through consensus.

(g) Evangelism by membership drive or by fellowship.

(h) Creative and effective forms of social involvement.

(i) New forms and uses for the connectional system of the Church.

(j) A salaried pastor or a worker-priest.

To help plan for the formation of a congregation, I invited thirty persons whom I had known in my work to a dinner meeting at a small, private dining room. When I arrived, the food line extended outside the building. When we finally got our food and moved into the eating area, it was packed with more than sixty persons present, half of whom I didn't know. After presenting the concept, I invited discussion. I had few answers for the questions that were asked; I only promised that together we would discover what the church of our day should be.

About forty persons decided to meet weekly in small groups and to come together on Sunday evenings to share insights. In the small groups, we first read the gospels, keeping in mind the question: "If Jesus walked our streets and called us to follow him today, what kind of church would he lead us to create?" Next, we read the book of Acts, asking, "If we received the Holy Spirit as did those early disciples, what kind of church would we create?"

By December, the group decided to meet in homes on Sunday morning. The form of those worship-study experiences grew out of our understanding of the essential nature of the church. In our three months of discussion, we had concluded certain things about the church:

■ It is a community of persons who have come into a right relationship with God through Jesus Christ.

■ It is a worshiping community.

■ It is a community which celebrates its life in the death and resurrection of Jesus Christ.

■ It is a missional community with a world concern.

■ It is a caring community, with the character of an extended family.

■ It is a community nurtured by teaching, proclamation, and the exercise of the gifts of ministry.

Next, we discussed ways to implement the elements which we had listed. Contracting with one another, each member committed himself to:

■ express himself honestly;

■ listen to each other person;

■ respond with feedback;

■ avoid blocks such as placating, blaming, intellectualizing, distracting, and withdrawing;

■ hang in with the community;

■ depend upon the Spirit of God to reveal himself in the feelings, desires, responses, and deeds of the people of God.

Through this process of sharing, listening, caring, and celebrating, the individual members of the community — without losing their own identity — become complementary parts of a whole — the whole Body of Christ.

This fellowship with God and with each other is the context for all aspects of the church's life — worship, mission, evangelism, organization, preaching, teaching, celebration. If you separate the dimension of fellowship from these other aspects, they become distorted; they become ends in themselves and they no longer minister to the needs of persons.

Let me share with you some of my expectations for this spiritual community.

I hope this spiritual community will be a carrier of the Spirit of God so that each week when I meet with my fellow Christians, I will encounter God both with them and through them. I really expect to hear God speak through their witness, through the reading of scripture, and through the prayers that are offered.

I seem to experience God in a very real way each week. I especially recall the Sunday morning when we looked at the meaning of faith. To help us feel dependency, we had a "blind trust walk." Each of us took a partner, and for five minutes one person pretended he was blind. Without speaking, the other introduced him to his world. After five minutes, the roles were reversed. I felt the wonder of being able to depend upon someone else to help me with my life.

The climax came when the leader played the pop record "Lean on Me." The community spontaneously formed a circle and began to swing with the music and to dance in celebration of God being alive in our midst.

I hope my spiritual being can be actualized in this community. To actualize my spiritual being, I need physical and emotional safety, love, a feeling of belonging, self-esteem, opportunities to express respect and appreciation for other persons, and encounters with the Spirit.

Through the meeting of my basic needs, I begin to actualize myself as a Spirit-inspired new creation. As I express the Spirit spontaneously, I feel celebration. I am on top of things; life seems worthwhile, exciting.

I recall that when we were studying the letter to the Ephesians, the leader gave each of us a piece of newsprint and a crayon. He asked us, in turn, to tape our newsprint to the wall and write on it affirming words given us by the other members of the congregation. When my turn came and I placed my newsprint on the wall, these affirmations of me were called out:

enthusiastic
friend
innovator
spiritual
understanding
leader
responsive
expansive

With these affirming words I felt loved, accepted, and important to this community. I moved to a new level of openness to the Holy Spirit, permitting him to break into my life, releasing my own spirit from within.

As I participate in this spiritual community, I hope to encounter other persons who are endeavoring to realize their hopes and dreams. At times, I forget that every person holds a secret dream for his life.

Once, while walking through the terminal of the Atlanta airport, I was struck by a flash of insight: "Each of these persons has a unique identity. Each entertains a secret hope for his life." There's a difference between my relationship with the masses who rub shoulders in the airport and my relationship with the small congregation to which I belong. I cannot hope to become acquainted with the hopes of the crowd, but in a fellowship I can get to know each person's deepest feelings and aspirations, and I can share in his efforts to become the person God wills him to be.

I hope to be understood and accepted and I need to understand and accept others. When I do not have a community off which to bounce half-formed ideas, it's hard for me to develop them. A friend stated, "I need a community of faith and love in which to test the ideas and impulses of my being. I need that place to practice my becoming." I hope this spiritual community will pick up my dream, understand it, evaluate it, and enlarge it with me.

As this community began to form, I recognized that most of the members had the wrong image of me. They knew me as Mr. Lay Witness Mission. Although I believe that God is using Lay Witness Missions in a magnificent way in the lives of thousands of persons, I recently have been having new experiences.

I have had doubts about my new roles and my ability to perform in my emerging life-style. I needed to verbalize these doubts to these significant persons, yet I felt anxious about telling them who I now understood myself to be. When I did tell them who I am today, I felt accepted. Because I felt safe, I was able to explore new needs and test new patterns of relating.

I hope to be with persons more mature than I am. I see them being authentically themselves, and their example stirs me to be more real. I see them acting with tremendous courage, and they inspire me to risk expressing myself.

I recall a man in our community who became dissatisfied with his vocation, although he was making more than $20,000 a year and had excellent prospects for advancement. He resigned because certain company policies did not meet his ethical standards. He did not have a job to move into. His courage has given me courage to risk vocational growth.

Finally, I hope the spiritual community will serve to correct both my dreams for the future and my actions in the present. I have a strong confidence in God's guidance through a community of faith. Quite literally, I believe that the assembled community is the Body of Christ, possessed with his Spirit. As these members act upon each other, they are communicators of the mind and will of God.

When we first formed the community, I sought approval from the United Methodist Church. The district superintendents responsible for the Atlanta area seriously questioned the proposal. Their reasons had very little to do with the nature of the congregation; rather, the concerns which they expressed were peripheral. For example, as we met for lunch, they gave four reasons for not constituting our house church as a United Methodist congregation:

1. We do not know who governs the Institute of Church Renewal, Inc., which employs you.
2. Lay witnesses do not make good churchmen.
3. You often speak as though you are anticlerical.
4. You are trying to form a new denomination.

From my perspective, these reasons seemed to be a cover-up. Had these been *real* reasons, I think I could have cleared up their objections. First, I could have given them a list of responsible board members. Second, I could have identified scores of lay witnesses who have made model churchmen! Third, I have often spoken out of anger about clergymen because I have been angry with myself for my phony role-playing. Fourth, I have no intention — not even a fantasy — of forming a new denomination.

When I reported this encounter to the community, a sensitive leader said, "Maybe God is trying to tell us something about the direction of our congregation. Possibly, there was a reason why we were not to be a United Methodist congregation." Although I do not yet know all the implications of this experience, I accept the fact that God is in it and he is working with us in ways which we do not, at this time, understand. So, I really believe that one day I will look back at this moment as a work of the Spirit of God through men. At the time, I thought that the superintendents, in blocking the test congregation, were also blocking the Spirit, but this may not be the case. This kind of resistance from spiritually sensitive persons may represent God's Spirit as clearly as positive affirmations do.

Just as I look to the community to help fill some of my needs, I also have a responsibility to the community. The community will form and develop only as each person takes responsibility for himself and becomes responsible to his brother. Let me elaborate:

■ The community will grow as I recognize and use the gifts which God has given me.

■ I have a responsibility to help other persons in the community recognize their gifts and utilize them for ministry.

■ In a community of such diverse persons, I must accept a variety of expressions of faith and commitment. Whereas I once felt that *agreement* was the measure of unity, I now believe that *understanding* and *acceptance* are more important.

■ I act responsibly when I recognize God in the midst of our fear, uncertainty, and struggle. I am unfaithful when I try to fit this group of persons into a preconceived form. I believe the God of history acts in our struggle, and responding to him is more important than creating the perfect church. Far better to be in a struggle to improve an imperfect community than to conclude falsely that we have arrived at Utopia.

Although I need a spiritual community for the actualization of my being, my actualization demands more than my individual expression and the responses of other persons. I need to participate in a community which has transcendent meaning, one that seeks to actualize the Kingdom of God in history. It must concern itself not only with my needs and the needs of my brother and sister inside the fellowship, but also outside our fellowship. This concern will lead the community to identify with the poor and the other powerless groups in the world.

God calls each of us to participate in making this world a place where spiritual actualizers can live out their being. That word — spoken to us through Jesus of Nazareth in his life, death, and resurrection, and carried through history by the Spirit in the spiritual community — still comes to us with beckoning urgency.

I hear that word and I respond from the depths of my being: "Yes, count me in! I want to be included in the call and to participate in the response!"

celebration,
the capstone of life

chapter 14

    You are somebody. You are a unique, unrepeatable miracle of God. As a unique person, you have unique needs, unique aspirations, unique resources. I hope that you are finding a new sense of freedom to be your unique self based upon the realization that your worth is a gift from God, not something that you earn.

My friend Maxie Dunnam closes his letters with "Keep on dancing." For most of his life, Maxie was plagued by self-doubt, but in recent years he has lived the celebrative life — dancing in the sun, dancing in the rain, dancing during growth, dancing during pain. The secret of life is to keep on dancing.[10]

Because I regard celebration to be the capstone — the finishing building block — of the free, open-style life, I am writing about it last. Of the new experiences which I have had, I'm proudest of my new freedom to celebrate life. Let me try to describe it.

Benjamin Christopher was a late arrival — he came eighteen years after Vange. When he was five days old, Betty and I began to think about a special christening service to celebrate his birth. We decided to baptize Chris on a Sunday afternoon. To enhance the spirit of celebration, we made the occasion a covered dish supper.

At five in the afternoon, about 100 friends arrived, bringing along with them tantalizing foods and festive spirits. The presence of relatives and close friends from distant places heightened our joy.

To open the celebration, I said to our guests: "The birth of Benjamin Christopher is a joyous occasion, and I am grateful that you are celebrating it with us. Too often, we separate our religious commitment from the joyous occasions of our lives, but today I am asking you, our friends, to join us in expressing gratitude to God and to rejoice with us in fellowship."

A dear friend, the Reverend W. Burney Overton, led us in a simple but extremely meaningful celebration of Christian baptism.

In preparation for this occasion, I had bought a large orange-and-red cup. Our neighbor Wayland Moore, a noted artist, printed on the cup the words "Cup of Blessing."

As part of the baptism ceremony, Burney dipped his fingers into the cup, which had been filled with water, and then placed his hand on Chris's head.

"Benjamin Christopher," Burney said, "I baptize you in the name of the Father, and of the Son, and of the Holy Spirit."

At the close of the baptism service, Burney replaced the water with wine. Then, following a few words of consecration, he broke bread and passed the bread and the wine-filled cup among the celebrating community. This use of the cup instilled meaning which I hope will increase with the years as we celebrate the new expressions of Chris's being.

I envision the "Cup of Blessing" becoming an increasingly important memorial in Chris's life. When he is a few years older, I can picture myself taking the cup and putting it in Chris's hands and saying to him, "Son, when you were a baby, friends came to our house to celebrate your birth. We thanked God for giving you to us, and we promised God that we would help you to grow up and be the kind of boy and man that he wants you to be. A good friend of ours took water from this cup and placed a few drops of it on your head. This was a way for us to say to God and to each other that we were all part of the Christian family, dedicated to God and to one another. On that occasion, I promised that when you got older, I would tell you what this happy time meant."

On this and other occasions, Chris and I can talk about the love of God and the love of friends, and what both mean in our lives. I can tell him that God has a purpose for each of us, and that we spend our lives learning what this purpose is and expressing it as we understand it.

When Chris is even older, I can tell him about the wine that was placed in his cup and passed among our friends. We can talk about Christ giving himself for us on the cross. We can talk about Jesus as both man and God, about his life example, and about his total acceptance of us as persons.

The cup will be used to celebrate other significant moments in Chris's life. For example, when he was nine months old, he took three steps. Chris sensed that he had achieved something important. His little face beamed. I rushed to the cabinet where the "Cup of Blessing" was stored. I took the cup and squeezed the juice of an orange into it. Then Chris, his mother, and I sat on the floor, sharing the juice and celebrating this new stage in Chris's development.

Chris won't be able to recall his "first-three-steps party" in specific terms, but he does happen to be an orange juice addict, so there will be some lingering feelings of pleasure. Later, I can tell him how we celebrated the occasion and how he registered his approval with loud smacking.

I anticipate getting down the cup when Chris speaks his first words, when he begins school, when he scores his first sports victory, etc. Who knows, we may use the cup to celebrate his engagement and, later, his marriage. And eventually, Chris may use the cup to celebrate a child of his own.

Now I do not, of course, intend to chart Chris' life activities for him. I do not intend to impose *my* devices — including the "Cup of Blessing" — upon him. He will live his own life; he will identify and celebrate those parts of it which have value for him. He will devise his own cups of blessing. Even so, I believe that these early celebrations with his family are important. When, as an adult, he plays back his childhood feelings and his parent tapes, I like to think that these celebrations will evoke warm responses which he can reaffirm and expand.

In the larger context of life, the "Cup of Blessing" demonstrates symbolically that life is to be celebrated, not merely endured; that the joyous episodes of life are to be fondly recalled, not noted and forgotten.

To celebrate life, I must first come alive. Then I can identify the high moments in my life — past and present — and place behind each of them an exclamation mark (where, in the past, I was accustomed to putting a period or question mark). This is no shallow exercise. Celebration enables me to fix significant moments more firmly in the meaning-center of my life. Instead of my life being a mishmash, it becomes a coherent unity. I can feel the connectedness of the meaningful events in my life.

Peak events, including baptism and marriage, demand to be saturated in the festive spirit. Embrace the event! Own it! Celebration catches up the past, present, and future, and it ties these dimensions of our lives together with a ribbon of meaning. To celebrate underscores the fact that life has purpose, direction, and unity.

Unfortunately, our technological age places exclamation marks behind the wrong things: the invention of an electric nail clipper; a rise in the Gross National Product; the purchase of a forty-foot boat to replace a thirty-six-foot boat. We've put our lives on "automatic pilot," and we've become so mesmerized by the whirring of its computers, instant feedback circuits, and efficient adjusting of our lives' trim tabs that we have lost the fine art of celebrating new actualizations of our being. We have applied to our personal lives the same automatic and detached processes by which we grind our coffee and cool our homes. We're so committed to mimicking the wheels of business and industry that if we dare to celebrate some simple, uneconomic happening, we may draw glances which say, "He ought to have his head examined."

So, we don't celebrate the richness of life; we dutifully chronicle "the tragic sense of life." Rather than look at life with hope, we view life with alarm. The net result is that we are a frozen people.

I believe that the loss of celebration in our lives comes in concert with our sense of a loss of God. Once we have relegated God to the sweet by and by, there is no way he can enter into the meaningful events of the present. Under these circumstances, for all practical purposes, "God is dead." I insist that we must recover celebration as a vital part of spiritual living. Celebration is biblical; it is also practical.

Of all the examples of the celebrative life which we find in the Bible, Jesus' last supper with his followers stands above the rest. I want to examine this celebration with you. Let's capture some of the important elements:

The background to the story is Jesus' declared intention to return to Jerusalem for the final time. On several occasions, he had shared with his disciples his sense of impending death. On the eve of this last trip into the city, he instructed a group of his followers to enter the city and make arrangements which he described. This they did.

Since the details of the last supper are familiar to you, let me move directly to the important elements of this model of Christian celebration.

First, Jesus recognized that this moment was a uniquely meaningful point in his ministry. For the past three years, he had anticipated his death, and now the time had come. He understood that by laying down his life, he was expressing both his own unique being and his identification with God. Celebration flows out of the recognition of meaning — *the depth of the celebration will be in proportion to the depth of the meaning.*

Second, Jesus deliberately punctuated this crucial time in the life of his community with a supper. Suppose that there had been no supper; suppose that, instead, the Jewish leaders had summarily captured Jesus, tried him, and crucified him. If this had happened, you and I would have been robbed of recognizing the meaning of these events and their symbolic content. On the contrary, Jesus ordered a celebration in a special place. His disciples recognized that they were not in the upper room through chance; they were there for a calculated experience together.

Third, Jesus symbolized this event in terms of common elements taken from the supper table. The profundity of the celebration lies in its simplicity. Common bread — "This is my body." Dinner wine — "This is my blood." Eating bread and drinking wine was a daily experience, and so Jesus used that common experience as a symbol to express the ultimate truth about God's relation to man.

The fourth vital element of this celebration was the instruction of Jesus, "Remember me as often as you partake of the bread and the wine." One central experience of the millions who have broken his body and drunk his blood is the recollection of his death and resurrection. The supper recalls the good news that God accepts us as unique persons of worth. Jesus meant for his followers to recall him and to reaffirm their own history. When I celebrate the Lord's Supper, I recall my Lord and sense his sustaining grace in my life.

A final element of this celebration is Jesus' promise, "I

will not share this celebration again until we drink it together in the Kingdom of God." In this promise, Jesus anticipates with his followers a future when the will of God will triumph in the lives of all persons. No matter how painful my present circumstances, I can take heart in the promise that God's love will triumph and I will sit with fellow Christians celebrating his kingdom. Paul underscored this future aspect of the Lord's supper celebration when he said, "And when you take it, remember the Lord's coming again." Celebration always contains hope and expectation.

Although I think that it is helpful for me to analyze celebration so that I can come to a more precise understanding of it, I must acknowledge the dimensions of celebration which cannot be captured in finite terms. These dimensions include spontaneity, fantasy, and ecstasy.

While mention of "celebration" popularly projects an image of a group of persons engaged in festivity together, celebration also has a high individual content. Celebration can be a solitary activity; even when it is corporate, each member of the group must identify the meaning of the event for himself and appropriate that meaning in personal terms. More and more, I am trying to open myself to the possibilities of solitary celebration arising spontaneously out of my sense of being. Often, this embraces fantasy and ecstasy.

Whatever the circumstances, celebration can arise only when I experience a new meaning in or for my life. I recall a team session at The Forum, which is sponsored by the Christian Laymen of Chicago. I sensed that some of my Chicago friends had developed an elevated image of me, seeing me as a deeply spiritual person and a powerful Christian. At their annual sessions, I felt compelled to strike the pose that they expected. As a result, I often came away feeling guilty because of my deception.

On my way to Chicago this particular year, I recognized that I was a different person from what they presumed me to be and I decided to risk showing the group who I really was. During the report session, I said, "I'm glad to be at The Forum this year. I bring with me uncertainty about myself and what I have to offer any of you. I am committing myself to be genuine with you, to share with you my honest feelings, and to let you deal with me in whatever way you desire."

There had been two celebrations. First, I had by myself celebrated a new level of meaning in my life, and then I had celebrated this growth with others in a caring, sharing community. Other redemptive celebrations followed as these men and I tried to be honest with each other.

Often, the celebrations in which I share mark someone else's joyful experience. One Sunday, a friend who was the local sales manager for a large paper company edged up to me before church and said, "I have some good news. I've just returned from a meeting in Boston at which the president of our company asked me to be vice-president in charge of marketing."

"Bob," I said, "I celebrate this occasion with you. Let's rejoice in the Lord together."

My good feelings arose chiefly out of my love for my friend, but I would be less than honest if I didn't acknowledge to you a sense of personal gratification as well. On many occasions, Bob had poured out to me his hopes for larger duties, and I had expressed confidence that his talents would be recognized. Although I had not contributed to his success in a direct way, I had invested myself in his situation. His promotion, then, held meaning for me and I appropriated it.

Even as I celebrate good fortune, I am aware that life is not one big, uninterrupted party. However, it is easier for me to accept and place in perspective the reverses of life when I look at them from the perspective of the goodness of life.

Let me picture what I mean. My daughter and I passed through a couple of painful years during which she was discovering her identity and I was trying to come to a better understanding of my role as her father. At times, we experienced suspicion, fear, and estrangement. But more recently, we have both come to a truer realization of who we are, and we are reaching out to each other. My spirit leaps for joy as I note that this relationship is being cemented. *Thank you, God, for this special gift. Never let me forget to celebrate it.*

140

Symbols, too, help me celebrate. A gift, for example, whether or not it has intrinsic value, carries a meaning — often an enduring one. Let me illustrate:

One Sunday as I arrived at church, Paul Coulter called to me, "Wait up, I want to talk to you." He came up to me holding out his hand. In it was a flat, brown stone. In a serious manner, he said, "Yesterday, while walking along the lakeshore, I saw this rock and it made me think of you, so I picked it up and brought it to you." He handed me the rock. I examined it as appreciatively as anyone can an ordinary rock, thanked him, and walked into church.

On Monday, I placed the rock on my desk. In the weeks that followed, I became increasingly aware of its presence. Paul had said that the rock reminded him of me — now the rock reminded me of Paul. This man was as humble as this rock and just as unchanging. No task was too menial. He was always dependable. And there was a direct word connection between this rock and Paul. Some of the men in the church had undertaken to clear the lawn of rocks, but all of them had tired of the chore except Paul. He spent Saturdays at this task until it was completed.

Paul's life and our relationship are worth celebrating, and the rock on my desk reminds me to celebrate. How long has this rock been on my desk? Twelve years!

As I look around me, I discover other gifts which stimulate my memory:

My grandfather's watch calls to my mind many happy days spent on his farm, riding his bulls, plowing his mule, driving his car.

A picture of three ships pulled up onto land ("High and Dry") reminds me of high and dry moments in the lay witness movement.

A New English Bible represents the team who staffed the National Clergy Conferences.

A boomerang speaks to me of the courage and commitment of Ron Barling, ICR director in Australia.

Each of these symbols is tied to a strand of experience; together, the strands form the fabric of my life. Usually, the meaning which the symbols convey to me today is less intense than was the original event itself. But there have been instances where the event held more meaning than I was able to appropriate at the moment — Paul's handing me that rock, for example.

Memories transcend the limitations of time and space, permitting my emotions to flow freely even when the event or person which evoked them is geographically remote, or even dead. Also, memories are transcendent in that they project a future to which I can relate and can anticipate with relish. Indeed, I am most miserable when I cannot conjure up a memory which holds sufficient personal meaning to motivate me to move out of myself and invest my attention and energies elsewhere. Often, I have cured my diseased spirit by engaging in celebration. Celebration gives me the *courage to be* in spite of discouraging circumstances.

A friend who had become a Christian in his early forties became an ardent lay witness. For several years, he exuded a contagious spirit of joy and excitement. Then he experienced a series of devastating events. He suffered a heart attack, which blocked him from going on Lay Witness Missions. And even as he lay abed recuperating from the heart attack, he learned via television that his father-in-law, a public figure, had died. A bit later, his mother-in-law discovered that she had terminal cancer. Recently, my friend recalled a conversation which he and I had during that dark stretch of time.

"You told me that there are times in our lives when we come up against mountains that we can't climb over — instead, we have to tunnel through them. As I've faced my mountains, I've found it's just as you said. Sometimes I find myself in a tunnel where I can't see light at either the entrance or the exit. When I find myself in this predicament, I think of my friends — people who really care about me. Their seeming presence with me warms my heart and illuminates my path. Soon I regain hope that I can make it."

There are times in my life when the spirit of celebration has evaporated. In such a time, I take the hands of my friends and the Lord. We walk together and soon life seems brighter. Again, I have reason to celebrate.

Jesus promised, "I will drink it with you in the Kingdom

of God." His promise assures our future. Today's meaningful encounters will, in that time of fulfillment, serve as souvenirs of our struggles and growth.

The hit play *Godspell* illustrates the celebrative aspect of the gospel — an aspect which often is lost to modern man. Some accuse the play of lacking reverence — for example, in dressing Christ like a harlequin and having him and Judas do a soft-shoe dance. I believe the deeper intent of the play underscores the gospel as celebration. Presenting the gospel in music, dance, and song can release a festive spirit which sermons, prayers, or confessions may not evoke.

For me, the celebration of life was most graphically depicted in the play's crucifixion scene when all the friends of Jesus writhed in agony with him. Before his final breath, they fell dead at the base of the restraining fence. When Jesus expired, each of them arose, one by one, and went to Jesus and took him down from the cross. As they lifted him above their heads, they danced around the stage singing, "God is alive, God is alive." While this is not the traditional depiction of the resurrection, it does present powerfully the meaning of the resurrection: that Christ is alive in our midst; that he is in us, living his life through us and giving us back our lives. Because he is alive in us, we sing, "God is alive . . . ."

Before the last sounds of the finale died, the audience was on its feet and applauding wildly. For ten minutes, the crowd seemed transfixed in the spirit of celebration.

Later, as I reflected on that drama, I felt sure that some persons heard the gospel of Christ in the context of celebration and responded as they might never have responded to a conventional interpretation. I would conjecture that the party which Matthew gave in honor of Jesus had the same festive spirit of celebration.

Celebration is the capstone of life. God created us to *live*, not to be *religious*. In each step of growth, we can count on the presence of the Holy Spirit to enable us. And each step calls for celebration in the Spirit.

I invite you to be a unique, unrepeatable miracle of God. This is God's intention; this is his gift. And this gift, my friend, is something to celebrate!

annotated bibliography

chapter 2 — WHAT'S IN MY POT?

    1. Satir, Virginia. *Peoplemaking.* Palo Alto, California: Science and Behavior Books, Inc., 1972.

        This book contains the "pot" analogy which I have elaborated upon and will be very helpful to readers seeking an in-depth analysis of personhood.

chapter 3 — THE OK GOSPEL

    2. Harris, Thomas A., M.D. *I'm OK — You're OK.* New York: Harper & Row, Publishers, 1967.

chapter 4 — WHO AM I PLUGGED INTO?

    3. Barnhart, Phil. *Don't Call Me Preacher.* Atlanta: Forum House, Inc., 1972.

        "The stepladder syndrome" is just one of the battles the author describes in this book written for "laymen and other ministers." He outlines candidly his search for authenticity in his relationships with God, himself, and his fellow man — plus his ministry in a changing neighborhood.

chapter 5 — LIVING FROM THE INSIDE OUT

    4. Maslow, Abraham H., ed. *Motivation and Personality.* New York: Harper & Row, Publishers, 1970.

       Maslow, Abraham H. *Toward a Psychology of Being.* New York: Van Nostrand Reinhold, 1968.

        Maslow's ideas about needs, developed in both these volumes, have influenced me tremendously.

chapter 8 — WHOSE VOICE DO I LISTEN TO?

5. Harris, pp. 38-59.

chapter 11 — OPEN LETTER TO A BRIDE

6. Reprinted from *The Prophet*, by Kahlil Gibran, with permission of the publisher, Alfred A. Knopf, Inc. Copyright 1923 by Kahlil Gibran; renewal copyright 1951 by Administrators C.T.A. of Kahlil Gibran Estate, and Mary G. Gibran.

7. O'Neill, Nena, and O'Neill, George. *Open Marriage, a New Life Style for Couples*. New York: M. Evans and Co., Inc., 1972.

The O'Neills develop a number of the principles which I have outlined. Although I do not agree with many aspects of this book, I believe that some readers will find it helpful.

8. Gibran, p. 16.

chapter 12 — WHEN FAMILY CONNECTIONS BREAK

9. Satir, Virginia. *Conjoint Family Therapy*. Palo Alto, Calif.: Science and Behavior Books, Inc., 1967.

In both this volume and *Peoplemaking* (previously cited), Virginia Satir offers valuable insight into the communications process.

chapter 14 — CELEBRATION, THE CAPSTONE OF LIFE

10. Dunnam, Maxie. *Dancing at My Funeral*. Atlanta: Forum House, Inc., 1973.

Maxie has written an unusual and thoughtful account of his spiritual struggles and triumphs. His ideas on authentic Christian living, gleaned from his own experiences, make for lively reading.